'Disorderly Order'

Colours in silent film

Published by Stichting Nederlands Filmmuseum
P.O. Box 74782
1070 BT Amsterdam
The Netherlands

© 1996 Stichting Nederlands Filmmuseum

Transcriptions: Patricia Jansma
Copy editor: Martin Joughin
Frame stills: Ole Schepp
Designed by: Menno Landstra A.A.
Printed by: Rob Stolk BV, Amsterdam

Distributed by British Film Institute - Book Publishing
21 Stephen Street
London W1P 1PL
Great Britain
fax: 44 1 71 4367950

ISBN 90-71338-09-6

DAAN HERTOGS & NICO DE KLERK

editors

'Disorderly Order'

Colours in silent film

The 1995 Amsterdam Workshop

CONTENTS

EDITORS' PREFACE

The Amsterdam Workshop

The Nederlands Filmmuseum seeks actively to pro-
mote its archival material for research purposes, and
this is one aim of the Amsterdam Workshop, founded in
1994. The Workshop focuses on issues and themes promi-
nent in the museum's preservation and programming activities, concentrating on areas that are relatively new or
neglected in film history, thereby hoping to extend the
subject matter and the approaches of current film-historical research.

The Workshop takes the form of a balanced combination of screenings and discussions. The importance accord-
ed to screenings of very diverse material reflects the
museum's open-minded archival philosophy, in which all
filmmaterial is considered valuable, independently of
generic and other classifications. To discuss the material
screened, a number of film scholars, film archivists, filmmakers, and experts from related fields are invited to the
museum to exchange their views. The first workshop, in
July 1994, was devoted to nonfiction from the teens.

Colours in silent film

The theme of the second Amsterdam Workshop
(26-29 July 1995) was colours in silent film. Our use of
the plural, 'colours', seems to us abundantly justified by
the variety of colours that adorned the films and film programmes of the silent era, by the various ways in which
these colours were applied to the film material, and (no
less importantly) by the various transformations these
colours have undergone and are still undergoing.

It may seem redundant to observe that a wide variety of
colours was used in silent films. Yet the occasional text
that addresses our 1995 theme rarely explores more than a
handful of the colours actually used in early cinema. One
reads in such texts that blue indicated night and red indicated love. Besides the general failure to differentiate, in
these associations, between referential and symbolic levels
of meaning, apart from the fact that such casual observations apply only to monochromatic images, and aside
from the fact that these two 'stereotypical' examples
betray a bias toward fiction films, this sort of remark tends

to suggest that other colours have equally straightforward meanings that the writer is unable - for reasons of space, in an introductory text, or whatever - to list in full. It would indeed be impossible to produce a comprehensive list, but not for such reasons. The two colours regularly cited are in fact the only ones that appear to have clearly identifiable associations - and these 'associations' may well be more statistical than semantic. A repeated exposure to identically coloured night and love scenes seems to trigger a desire for systematicity, even though this bare repetition may be the limit of any 'system of colour' in silent film. For blue and red are also to be found beyond the confines of night and love, and such 'divergent' occurrences are far from statistically insignificant. Another limitation of such casual observations is that they identify cinematic colour exclusively as an element in the production of meaning in a single film. But in the silent era, or certainly during the first two decades of film history, the film programme was probably a far more natural unit than the individual film. The variation of colouring a programme and its component films, the rhythms of such variation, may well be more significant than any specific 'meaning' attributable to any particular colour.

The silent era witnessed innumerable attempts, applying widely varying levels of technical sophistication, to show films in colours. Such attempts fall into two major categories: 'natural' or photographic methods depending on the mechanical combination of two or three differently coloured but otherwise identical monochrome images on the celluloid or screen (in systems such as Kinemacolor, Dufaycolor and Kodacolor, to mention some better-known examples), and applied colour methods, in which a black-and-white print was treated in some way with coloured dyes after photographic processing. The applied colour systems comprise hand-painting, stencilling, toning and tinting. The Workshop focused mainly on these techniques, partly because they are far better represented than early photographic colour in the archive of the Nederlands Filmmuseum, but perhaps more importantly - a virtue of this necessity - because they jointly present the full range of early colouring from black-and-white and the varieties of whole-image monochrome to complex local and multiple colours. Hand-painted and stencilled images, owhich are particularly resistant to casual or stereotypical interpretations of early coloured film, have too often been overlooked or marginalized in early film history. To disregard stencil colouring is, moreover, virtually to disregard an entire genre - the *féerique* - and a significant part of the output of such studios as Pathé and Gaumont.

The variety in colours found on early films is also, finally, a result of their instability. The Nederlands Filmmuseum has a certain reputation for its preservations of silent coloured films. But no preservation process is 'perfect' (whatever exactly that might mean to different people) and we wanted, among other things, to demonstrate to participants of the Workshop (and eventually, to readers of this book) that any process of preserving coloured film on acetate saftey stock tense to depart in some measure from the applied colours on the original nitrate prints. We also wished to emphasize that there is more than one way to preserve coloured film and that each method has specific advantages and limitations as a way of reproducing applied colours. The choice of methods partly determines, for example the extent to what, an archivist or technician can choose between reproducing colours as they now appear on the nitrate *or* as they are thought to have appeared when the nitrate print was in circulation. This consideration itself reflects the fact that applied colours have, from the time of their initial application to the black-and-white positive print, been subject to unrelenting changes occasioned first by the wear and tear of projection in the silent era and then by ageing and decay in the vaults of film archives.

Discussion of this 'final change' at the Amsterdam Workshop has in fact already prompted a significant development that may considerably reduce the gap between archival nitrates and modern acetate copies. Two Workshop participants, Paul Read and John Sears of Soho Images in London, were inspired by the 1995 discussions to revive and, more importantly, commercially exploit early colouring processes making them generally available for the first time since the silent era. Returning to contemporary sources, notably the technical and trade press of the period, they proceeded on the basis of much new information to undertake chemical analysis of the applied colour on nitrate stock. The first samples of the results so far obtained in their attempts to duplicate early methods were recently screened and looked very promising, presenting a range of colour effects far wider than that obtainable with the two standard modern methods. When their 'early' processes are fully developed, film archives will have a valuable new resource for the preservation of coloured nitrate prints.

The main text below, recording the Workshop discussions opens with a record of the introductions and discussions. When a session opened with a film programme, a list of the titles screened precedes it. Next, a moderator proposed topics for discussion on the basis of the material that had been screened. Participants were then invited to contribute their own reactions and views. The second part is a paper, written from an archival viewpoint. This essay takes as its point of departure the finiteness of our nitrate film heritage, in particular its colours. The essay takes up the question of how to consider the preservations of nitrate prints at a time, in the not too distant future, when the 'originals' themselves will be lost (and which, for almost all practical purposes, already are inaccessible).

Working from a transcript of the taped discussions, we have sought here to present a record of the Workshop proceedings in readable form, excluding some digressions and removing some of those characteristic divergences of spoken from written language that might distract the reader from the flow of argument. We hope the result does full justice to the welcome diversity of individual voices and perspectives that enlivened another year's debates at Amsterdam.

NEDERLANDS FILMMUSEUM
Daan Hertogs & Nico de Klerk
May 1996

PART I:

THE 1995 AMSTERDAM WORKSHOP
I N T R O D U C T I O N

Screening and Discussion

The main programme of the second Amsterdam Workshop consisted of three morning and three afternoon sessions during which a total of over a hundred films or film excerpts, selected from the Nederlands Filmmuseum archives, were shown to an invited audience of archivists, film historians, filmmakers and film technicians. The Workshop is conceived not only as a showcase for representative selections from the Amsterdam archive, but also as a stimulus to debate, and the museum invited six moderators to chair the discussions that followed each screening:

❖ Session 1 - **Giovanna Fossati**, from the Università di Bologna, was between January and August 1995 assistant researcher at the Nederlands Filmmuseum, where her research formed an essential input for the 1995 Workshop and its programme.

❖ Session 2 - **Don McWilliams** is a Canadian filmmaker who has directed a feature length documentary about Norman McLaren, CREATIVE PROCESS (1990). He is currently making for the National Film Board of Canada THE PASSER-BY, a live-action and animation found footage film.

❖ Session 3 - **Tom Gunning** teaches film history at Northwestern University, Evanston, USA. He is the author of *D.W. Griffith and the Origins of American Narrative Film* (1991), and of numerous articles on avant-garde cinema, early cinema, and the wider context of early film history.

❖ Session 4 - **Jacques Aumont** teaches aesthetics and film analysis at the Université de Sorbonne Nouvelle and directs the Collège d'Histoire et de l'Art Cinématographique at the Cinémathèque Française. His recent books include *L'oeil interminable, cinéma et peinture* (1989), *Du visage au cinéma* (1992), *Introduction à la couleur* (1994), and *La couleur en cinéma* (1995).

❖ Session 5 - **Peter Delpeut** is a Dutch filmmaker and was, at the time of the Workshop, deputy director and programmer of the Nederlands Filmmuseum. His recent work includes the found footage films LYRICAL NITRATE (1990) and THE FORBIDDEN QUEST (1992), and THE TIME MACHINE (1996), a three-hour television programme on the history of our visual culture.

❖ Session 6 - **Mark-Paul Meyer**, head of the Preservation Department of the Nederlands Filmmuseum, chaired the final session - a review of work on colour preservation in commercial and archival laboratories jointly presented by **Paul Read** (Soho Images, London), **Noël Desmet** (Koninklijk Filmarchief / Cinémathèque Royale, Brussels), **Mario Musumeci** (Centro Sperimentale di Cinematografia, Rome), and **Nicola Mazzanti** (Cineteca del Comune di Bologna, Bologna)

The programme of the 1995 Amsterdam Workshop was compiled by Daan Hertogs, head of the Research Department of the Nederlands Filmmuseum, and Giovanna Fossati. Daan Hertogs also chaired the 1995 Amsterdam Workshop.

The moderators had, over a preparatory weekend in May 1995, viewed all the films to be screened at the July Workshop, and each was asked to open their session with a short introductory survey of issues they wished the Workshop to address. As the choice of material screened was limited by the NFM collection, the screenings made no claim to present a comprehensive survey of coloured silent film; but by drawing on the specialist knowledge and experience of the moderators, the Workshop organizers were able in some degree to balance or compensate practical limitations on the amount and variety of material that could be shown. The choice of moderators (and the participation of others) from a range of different backgrounds also ensured that the Workshop discussions would cover a wide spectrum of different perspectives.

The evening screenings that closed each day's formal schedule complemented the daytime screenings and discussions by presenting a selection of coloured feature films from the NFM archive. The evening film programmes may be found in the overview of the Workshop schedule in the first appendix.

The record of the proceedings in each session is opened by a list of the films (or excerpts from films) screened in that part of the programme. Titles of NFM prints are given in the following order: print title; English translation of the print title; original title (when known). As the English titles are literal translations of the print titles, they sometimes depart from the original title. The list of films specifies furthermore whether a print is in black-and-white and/or coloured, including the colour system(s) used; when a print contains sequences combining colouring systems simultaneously, this is indicated by '+' (for instance, 'tinting + stencil'). If original titles or English translations of films from previous sessions are used in the text, notes give the print title.

We would request that any future references to the films should include their Nederlands Filmmuseum print titles.

Film programme:

STATION EN PANORAMA VAN CONWAY CASTLE / STATION AND PANORAMIC VIEW OF
CONWAY CASTLE / CONWAY CASTLE - PANORAMIC VIEW OF CONWAY ON THE L. &
N.W. RAILWAY ❖ Great-Britain (British Mutoscope & Biograph) 1898 ❖ D5812-X -
43m ❖ hand painting

FEEENDANS / DANCE OF THE FAIRIES / LA RUCHE MERVEILLEUSE ❖ France (Pathé)
1905 Dir. Gaston Velle ❖ DK342 - 58m (original print length 75m) / video 076 - 4'
[hand painting or stencil]

exerpt from: DE MOOISTE WAAIERS TER WERELD / THE MOST BEAUTIFUL FANS IN
THE WORLD / - ❖ France [1927] ❖ DK541 - 201m video / 202 - 10' ❖ stencil

DE MOEDIGE DOCHTER VAN DEN STATIONSCHEF / THE STATION MASTER'S COURA-
GEOUS DAUGHTER / THE LONEDALE OPERATOR ❖ United States of America
(Biograph) 1911 Dir. D.W. Griffith ❖ DK1384 - 286m / video 186 - 14'
black-and-white, tinting

AAN HET PARADIJSACHTIGE IRISCHE MEER / ON THE PARADISIACAL IRISH SEA / -
[France / Great-Britain (Eclair/Tyler) 1910] ❖ DK1973 - 47m / video 228 - 2'
toning

DE MOLENS DIE JUICHEN EN WEENEN / WINDMILLS THAT CHEER AND WEEP / L'AME
DES MOULINS ❖ The Netherlands-France (Hollandsche Film) 1912 Dir. Alfred
Machin ❖ DK1964 - 129m (original print length 180m) ❖ stencil, tinting + stencil,
toning + tinting

JOHANN STRAUSS / *idem* / *idem* ❖ [United States of America 1930 Dir. James A.
Fitzpatrick] ❖ DK1148 - 136m / video 109 - 5' ❖ [pre-tinting or tinting]

Moderator **Giovanna Fossati**: Programme notes are maybe appropriate, out-
lining the technology used to colour silent films as well as the technology
involved in the reproduction of their colours today. In other words, how were
nitrate prints coloured in the silent era and how are these colours preserved on
safety stock at the Nederlands Filmmuseum? These questions must be addressed
at the outset, since highly inflammable nitrate stock cannot be projected. Most of
the acetate projection copies to be screened during the course of the workshop
come from the NFM archive and most of these have been preserved by the NFM.
    When an NFM nitrate print is sent to the laboratory, a Kodak colour internega-
tive print is produced from which a positive print is made on colour stock. The

aim is to reproduce as closely as possible the colours on the nitrate. But the colours on the safety copy never exactly reproduce those on the nitrate, owing to the technical limitations of the processing currently available. These limitations derive in part from present-day colour stock - which for the internegative means present-day Kodak stock since no other manufacturer produces colour internegative material - and preservation techniques. But there are also financial constraints: we must usually make do with the first positive safety print produced at the lab, as long as the colour is 'satisfactory', which is a fairly loose criterion. The initial print usually becomes the final print, rather than just an answer print on which to base the colour adjustment in the final print.

Now consider the nitrates themselves. It has been estimated that between 1895 and 1930 something like eighty percent of films were projected in something other than plain black-and-white. The films were hand-coloured, mechanically coloured using stencils, tinted or toned, and the various techniques were often combined in a single film. These four techniques had one thing in common: the colouring was done on the black-and-white positive print. This sets such colouring apart from the techniques, already available in the teens, that attempted to reproduce colour by photographic means. As nearly all the films to be screened here were originally coloured by applying dyes to a positive print, I will confine myself to the basic techniques. The order I will follow isn't strictly chronological, since these techniques coexisted from the earliest phase.

Hand-colouring involves applying transparent aniline dyes to certain areas of the black-and-white image. This was done manually, frame by frame, with a brush. The method had been used over the second half of the nineteenth century to colour still photographic images, such as those projected with a magic lantern. As early as 1894-95 some of Edison's Kinetoscope films were hand-coloured, but the method became fairly uncommon after 1906. Hand-colouring can be identified by the flickering of coloured areas of the image, since the paintbrush could not produce very precise contours frame after frame. In most archives these hand-coloured nitrate prints are preserved by being transposed to colour internegative stock from which a positive colour print is made.

Stencil colouring involves a two-step process. First, the stencil must be made from a positive print where the area to be coloured in each frame is cut out; each colour requires a separate stencil - usually no more than six were used. The prints used as stencils must exactly match the black-and-white projection prints to be coloured, with excised areas in the stencil corresponding exactly to the appropriate shapes in the eventual projection print. After each stencil is cut, the photographic emulsion is washed from its surface to provide a clean and inert celluloid template. The cutting was initially performed manually, but between 1907 and 1910 the process was mechanized by using a pantograph. A technician traced out the area to be excised on a magnified projection of each frame, and the pantograph relayed this tracing movement to a needle which cut out the corresponding area in a positive print with a sort of sewing-machine action.

The second step in the process was to colour each projection print with the sequence of different stencils prepared in this way, one stencil for each colour.

Initially this also was done manually, with a brush, but the process was subsequently mechanized, using an apparatus in which the stencil, aligned with the black-and-white reel that would eventually become a projection print, passed under a velvet loop or pad constantly fed with dye. Individual stencils were of course used to colour several projection prints; after each run through the colouring apparatus, the stencils were washed before being re-used. We only have a reasonably complete documentation of how the work changed over the years in the case of Pathé, and it is not always easy to differentiate between stencilling and hand-colouring on a nitrate: it is quite difficult to determine whether, say, DANCE OF THE FAIRIES was hand-coloured or manually stencilled. But THE MOST BEAUTIFUL FANS IN THE WORLD was clearly stencilled mechanically. Here, the colours are extremely precise but sometimes 'out of shape' because the extensive movements made it more difficult to follow the shapes here than in less 'dynamic' fashion films.

Stencilled films are preserved, like hand-coloured films, by being copied onto a colour internegative from which a positive colour print is made. It is not always possible to reproduce all the colours on the nitrate since some colours, especially 'warmer' magentas, pinks and so on, are sometimes too faint to register on the colour internegative without distorting the overall spectrum. This is simply a problem with current Kodak colour internegative stock.

Tinting in its simplest and most common form is pretty much like dying clothes. A strip of film is immersed in a solution of aniline dye. Although the film emerges uniformly dyed, only the white areas in each frame - the transparent areas of the processed gelatine emulsion from which all the silver has been removed - transmit the colour of the dye. The blacks remain black, transmitting no light before or after absorbing the dye, while the intermediate greys are tinted in various degrees. Tinting therefore reduces contrast, and a black-and-white positive that is to be tinted should be printed with higher contrast than a positive intended for black-and-white projection.

Toning is a sort of converse process, or range of processes, in which the print to be coloured is bathed in a chemical solution that either converts the black silver in the emulsion directly in a differently coloured material or into a material which fixes coloured dye when the treated print is subsequently immersed in a dye solution. The density of the new colour depends on the amount of silver or darkness in any particular area of the original black-and-white image.

Tinted or toned nitrates are preserved, like hand-coloured or stencilled films, by transferring the image to a colour internegative then taking a positive print. By constantly referring to the original nitrate, one tries to obtain a spectrum as close as possible to the tinting or toning on the nitrate, though, as I have already noted, the nature of modern positive and internegative colour stock makes an exact reproduction almost impossible. It is very difficult, for example, to reproduce the difference between tinting and toning on safety stock, since the colours produced by nitrate tinting in the whites tend to be lost in the NFM process of transfer to safety stock. Thus an NFM acetate reproduction of a tinted nitrate has the same 'white' whites as a toned nitrate. Another problem is that the 'black-

and-white' of colour stock isn't really black and white, since the black always has a blue or brown 'tone'.

Tinting and toning were sometimes combined in one strip of film - tinting was also sometimes combined with stencilling. Thus, in WINDMILLS THAT CHEER AND WEEP, a sunset scene has been toned blue then tinted pink. The darker areas are variably toned and the lighter areas tinted, giving a blue landscape under a pink sky. The preservation of this shot posed the problem we encounter preserving the pinks in stencilled films: it's sometimes impossible to transfer very light pink tinting to acetate stock without unacceptably distorting the colour in toned areas.

Toward the end of the twenties - the beginning of the sound era - colouring positive prints became less common. Tinting and toning were said to interfere with the optical soundtrack laid down on the initial black-and-white positive print, but manufacturers introduced new dyes to reduce this effect, along with pre-tinted positive stock. The problem is in fact completely removed in our preservation process by transferring the soundtrack of tinted talkies onto black-and-white negative stock, while the images are copied onto colour internegative stock. So maybe today we have better sound than the original audiences.

Film programme:

LES SIX SOEURS DAINEF / THE SIX DAINEF SISTERS / LES SIX SOEURS DAINEF [France (Pathé)] 1902 ❖ DK1266 - 55m / video 143 - 3' ❖ [hand painting or stencil]

EEN VERVALLEN GROOTHEID / A DECLINING CELEBRITY / THE MASTER PAINTER United States of America (Vitagraph) 1913 ❖ DK377 - 298m / video 076 - 15' tinting, toning, black-and-white

NARREN-GRAPPEN / JOKES OF THE JESTER / [THE JESTER] ❖ [United States of America (Edison) 1908] ❖ DK1039 - 103m [original print length 900ft] / video 051 - 5' ❖ black-and-white, tinting

THE GREAT TRAIN ROBBERY / *idem* / *idem* ❖ United States (Edison) 1903 Dir. Edwin S. Porter ❖ DK1363 - 212m (original print length 230m) / video 159 - 11' [hand painting or stencil]

exerpt from: VERVLOEKT ZIJ DEN OORLOG / DAMNED BE WAR / MAUDITE SOIT LA GUERRE ❖ France-Belgium (Belge Cinéma Film) 1914 Dir. Alfred Machin DK825 - 860m / video 007 - 44' ❖ stencil, tinting, tinting + stencil

BITS & PIECES NO.209 / *idem* / - ❖ United States of America [1920] ❖ DK1404 - 40m / video 299 - 2' ❖ solarization

MESSTER WOCHE / MESSTER WEEKLY / MESSTER WOCHE ❖ Germany-Austria
(Messter) [1915] ❖ DK1090 - 179m / video 069 - 10' ❖ solarization

DE HYDRAULISCHE SLUIS TE PETERSBOROUGH, ONTARIO / HYDRAULIC LOCKS IN
PETERSBOROUGH, ONTARIO / - ❖ Great-Britain (Butcher & Sons) 1911 ❖ DK281 -
113m (original print length 126m) / video 118 - 6' ❖ toning + tinting

LA BELLE AU BOIS DORMANT / THE SLEEPING BEAUTY / LA BELLE AU BOIS DORMANT
France (Pathé) 1908 Dir. [Albert Capellani/Lucien Nonguet] ❖ DK1428 - 230m
(original print length 300m) / video 224 - 12' ❖ toning, stencil, toning + stencil,
tinting + stencil

BITS & PIECES NO.182 / *idem* / PHANTOM OF THE OPERA ❖ United States of
America (Universal) 1925 ❖ DK960 - 85m / video 011 - 5' ❖ two-colour
Technicolor

HET ALHAMBRA / THE ALHAMBRA / - ❖ [France, 1926] ❖ DK1968 - 127m / video
360 - 7' ❖ tinting, stencil

Moderator **Giovanna Fossati**: I would like to open the discussion in this session by adopting the perspective of an archivist. Although I cannot really
claim to be an archivist, spending seven months at the Nederlands Filmmuseum
viewing coloured archival material and thinking about it made me see things from
this perspective.

This session differs in format from those that will follow. After an hour of film
constantly interrupted by very clinical data, we were eventually allowed to enjoy a
second good hour of uninterrupted film. The first part of this session carefully
demonstrated the various colour systems and the techniques of colour preservation. The films themselves served simply as examples of that. But films aren't
usually made as examples of these things, so we had to cut them to fit this
purpose. But then we turned things around, so the films temselves ran the game,
the game of colours. The game is played with a knowledge of how colour was put
on the nitrate film, and a knowledge of how the colour of the nitrate print has
been restored to make it visible to a contemporary audience. The point of the
game is to combine these elements.

Why are we bothering with technical matters at all? Some people want technical
information about what they are seeing, but some probably don't. They can all
equally enjoy the films, of course, with or without this knowledge. But if you
want that information, whether as a simple matter of taste or for archival reasons,
what can you actually do with it, given the severe limitations on such knowledge?
As we have already seen, the colours on a safety print are different from those on
the nitrate prints; pink colours, for example, disappear, or tinting on the nitrate
looks like toning in the acetate. And of course the colours have changed on the
nitrate too, as in BITS AND PIECES NO. 209 which might have begun black-and-

white before becoming solarized and thus coloured. Some colours have faded through the years, as in MESSTER WEEKLY where the yellow patches may be faded yellow tinting. And even if a nitrate still has its original colours, we can't now see it properly projected - in the right projector with the right lamp and so on.

Let's take DAMNED BE WAR as an example of all this. It's a stencilled film, but one shot in the farewell sequence is black-and-white. Some of us may not even have noticed that shot, some may have found the black-and-white image very appropriate to the dramatic content of the scene; someone familiar with preservation might have wondered whether this black-and-white fragment had come from a black-and-white copy, because the fragment was missing in the coloured print. Three different responses: here in fact the 'correct' response is the third. The fragment does come from a black-and-white copy. But some day, any proof that this is the right answer may have disappeared. What could we say then? Of course, a codified documentation of the colour restoration should always be available. But that documentation would state the condition of the colours in, say, 1995, which still leaves eighty or ninety years of unknown territory. Or consider again MESSTER WEEKLY: we don't know where the yellow patches came from. Maybe some sort of scientific analysis would tell us whether it is faded yellow tinting or solarized blue, or solarized black-and-white, or who knows what. But where can we get that analysis and do we really need it, in fact?

Now, if we can't actually reproduce the colours on the nitrate, and can't even say how they will look a year from now, why are we preserving them at all? Maybe we just like them. If that is the answer, does it mean that we can just forget how the colours were produced and how precisely or imprecisely they can be preserved? Is a technical knowledge of any real use to us, given its great limitations?

Let us try to find another perspective. Today we may like the colours in a rather similar way to the way people liked them originally. We probably have the same vague awareness of the colours we see now as the original audience had of theirs. Or maybe we should rather say that early audiences had not so much a vague awareness of colour, but an awareness that colours are vague. This is in fact fairly clear from the technical manuals of the teens and twenties. In one such manual David Halfish writes in 1915: 'staining'[1] of a print is done in the washroom as a part of the washing process, and is done in the same manner that a laundress blues her clothes' - which is not a very technical statement. Or as Frederick Talbot writes: 'The circumstance that aniline dyes have to be used is a distinct handicap owing to their fugitive nature. The colours during the first runs through the projector are brilliant, but repeated exposure to the intense electric arc tones them down to a remarkable degree. In the end, the film tints have a washed-out appearance which is far from pleasing.' Carl Gregory writes in 1920: 'In no case where instructions are carefully followed, will the toned image deteriorate during the active life of the film.' But what is the active life of a film? We do not know, and nor did he. Maybe the instability of the colours is already inscribed in their genesis and we are stumbling over the myth of the original which can be reproduced over and over again while always remaining the same. But if that is not the case with preserva-

1. The contemporary term for tinting

LA BELLE AU BOIS DORMANT (Session 1) *nitrate*

LA BELLE AU BOIS DORMANT *acetate*

DE MOLENS DIE JUICHEN EN WEENEN (Session 1) *nitrate*

DE MOOISTE WAAIERS TER WERELD (Session 1) *nitrate*

tion today, as we saw in the first part of this session, and was not the case yesterday when the colours were applied - as we see from technical manuals, there may indeed be some use knowing about the old technologies of applying colour, even if it is doomed to be an incomplete, limited knowledge. We can use it as a theoretical base for the application of a contemporary technology of colour preservation, even though technologies, old and new, produce results that are vague and unstable, and both have to be inscribed in the history of a film.

Jacques Aumont: Doesn't the idea of preserving a film as preserving something in the process of decay also apply to what curators of paintings in museums are doing and have been doing for centuries, and especially since the last century? Of course, the decay of colours in paintings is much slower, but there are already similar problems to be faced in the preservation of nineteenth-century blacks. In paintings, we know that black is turning into something rather indeterminate. We know that the chrome yellow in a Van Gogh is fading or turning green. So, from an aesthetic or theoretical or more general point of view, is there a different problem in preserving a print or considering the evolution of the colour in a film, than considering the evolution of colour in a painting? Isn't this the general problem that images have a life of their own, however short or long?

Giovanna Fossati: The main difference is that with film, you have the nitrate print and you copy it onto different material. Our contemporary stock has the same 35mm format and the same perforations, but it is a different material. The silver emulsion on the nitrate is simply not there on coloured safety stock. You are copying aniline colours applied with a brush onto material which itself has three intrinsic layers of colour. With paintings you work on the actual painting.

Eric de Kuyper: To reply to Jacques Aumont's question, there is a great but very simple difference between cinema and paintings. With paintings, people have always been conscious of the need for preservation, of colours especially. People have been conscious of Van Gogh's yellow as Van Gogh's yellow from the start. That is the enormous difference with cinema and film history, and we have to explain this difference. The explanation is that we have only recently started to wonder about the bearing on film preservation of the fact that silent films were also coloured. For an older generation of archivists this was simply no problem: old films, silent films, were black-and-white. So it is a very new problem for us, which marks a major difference between painting and its old problematic of preservation, and film preservation. It has an ideological, aesthetic aspect.

Daan Hertogs: Although it is a new problem, the original nitrate was always there. The older generation of archivists sorted through coloured nitrate films for black-and-white preservations, and I don't believe this was just a question of money. My problem is that while preserving nitrate coloured film in black-and-white, they never stressed the fact that the original material was coloured.

Eric de Kuyper: I can cite a very good example. Jacques Ledoux of the Belgian film archive was very interested in the technical aspects of preservation. When I discovered that silent films were coloured I asked him 'Why don't you preserve them in colour?' And he answered with a *boutade*: that colour was like '*un groulot qui accompagne le trot du cheval*' - the ringing of the bells that accompany a trotting horse. For that generation it was not a problem. Not a financial, economic problem, not even a technical one. The question simply didn't arise, and we must wonder why.

Ansje van Beusekom: It goes back to the question: What is film? How did people understand film? Colour was something added later, and the purists wanted ed to cut out all these additions; Jacques Ledoux was raised in the tradition that early film is black-and-white.

Mark-Paul Meyer: Archivists are constantly confronted with the problem of whether they should preserve a film just as they find it - in this case, whether to restore the colours. Of course, more knowledge of the techniques of the teens and twenties would be a great help in restoring these films. The general approach of archives has been, and still is, to restore the print as found in the vaults. The questions for the scholars are: should we restore the colours; should we do research on the faded dyes; and when a film or a shot was blue but has become black-and-white, should we give it a new blue tinting? These are the questions archivists have to deal with all the time. And I would like to know what scholars think: should we preserve these films just as we find them, or should we try to get as close to the original as possible?

Tom Gunning: One of the issues here, the difference between film and painting, turns precisely on the idea of a unique original - physically unique - which is there in painting, but probably not in film. For Walter Benjamin, the difference was that the traditional arts had the aura of such unique originals, but the mechanically reproduced arts didn't, and he felt in fact that this was a revolutionary aspect of art in the modern age. What is interesting now, after another fifty, sixty years of film, is that we approach it as preservationists. We begin to feel there's something rather unique about certain prints, which ought to be preserved. But we're still stuck in a kind of paradox, because what are we preserving? We have a different mindset from say twenty or even forty years ago, when a film was supposed to have a kind of unique, aesthetic essence. Now we have the idea that a film has many variants, that it is important to look at different prints, and that a number of things, which were considered just simple additions, are now increasingly considered important. Musical accompaniment, for instance, has become more and more important. Part of the paradox is that maybe it's an impossible quest for historians to try to get back , not so much to the original object, as to the original experience. It's very interesting when people see colour, they very often ask 'How did the audience experience it?' Which, of course, we don't know. There's a sense of wanting to completely recreate a film. It's a fine ambition, fuelling so much research and knowledge, but it's somewhat paradoxical, because what we're trying to recreate is something that can never be completely recreated.

To respond to Mark-Paul Meyer's question, my feeling as a scholar, bracketing money issues, is that ideally I would like both his alternatives: for the print to be preserved with all the marks of time and history on it as a unique object, and at the same time for there to be another print that we would try in some sense to restore. Preservation and restoration are both important, though preservation is probably primary.

Sabine Lenk: Mark-Paul Meyer's question is very difficult, because as a historian working in an archive, I'd like to get as close as possible to the original. You could use the manuals produced by Kodak, Gevaert, Agfa, Pathé, which often give samples of colours, in order to get as close as possible to the original colours. But what is 'the original' if, as so often, you have several prints? Watching these films today, it was sometimes a relief to see parts in black-and-white, because these colours all the time can get very tiresome. The problem is that colours, especially tinting, leave a very hazy image, and I find myself wanting sharper contrasts. Sometimes, seeing a very sharp black-and-white picture is like relaxing my eyes.

Daan Hertogs: One important thing that Giovanna Fossati mentioned was the consciousness that when the original colours were applied, they were not meant to last. In other words, from the very beginning colours were condemned to a process of decay. So we should ask ourselves how the technical knowledge of the teens and twenties can be used for researching these films.

Peter Delpeut: Sabine Lenk also mentioned something important, which is taste. Can our personal appreciation of colour - what we like or don't like - be introduced into the discussion? I'd like to ask Mark-Paul Meyer, for example, whether he's ever tempted in a preservation just to bring in a colour he likes, and to say: why bother about authenticity, it makes a beautiful print?

Mark-Paul Meyer: Sometimes we do something like that. Often you know, or you have a quite clear idea, about the colour a scene should be, but sometimes you have to guess and invent. In DAMNED BE WAR, for instance, we decided not to colour a black-and-white sequence. First, because the context of the sequence was stencilled and we could not of course apply the stencilled colours frame by frame; secondly, just before the sequence there was a black-and-white photograph, and we thought it wouldn't be too visually disturbing to leave the black-and-white. But a later sequence in the film, the throwing of the bombs from the airplane, comes from the same black-and-white print, and we tinted it blue, because the immediately preceding and succeeding shots were blue. We also added colour in various other places, because you appreciate the film better when you're not being disturbed by black-and-white fragments.

Karel Dibbets: Peter Delpeut has actually posed a non-historical question by asking about our personal appreciation of colour. For me this non-historicity makes the question particularly attractive, and my primary response is that our appreciation of black-and-white is enhanced by our appreciation of colour. The problem of colour is really more a problem of the absence of colour in black-and-white. So we should invert the questions, and rather than asking about colour appreciation, ask how we appreciate black-and-white. It is much more interesting to consider why a film was presented in black-and-white. I'm suggesting a detour via the wider appreciation of black-and-white to an analysis of colour.

Thomas Elsaesser: What struck me from this viewing was the diversity, not so much of the techniques, but of the functions of colouring. It opens up so many ways in thinking about how colour can create specific effects - and they are, so often, very specific to the film in question. Obviously, the archivist must also be guided by an appreciation of the uses to which colour is put, as well as the aesthetic effects that can be achieved.

What is emerging in the discussion so far are very different agendas - and very interestingly different agendas. The agenda that Jacques Aumont alluded to, in talking about the life of the image, is one that many of us now feel with peculiar acuity, because it has imposed itself with the emergence and proliferation of electronic images. In other words, as soon as you have the technical ability to modify the image to the degree that we now can modify digitized images, the life of celluloid takes on an entirely different historical significance. The life of colour on celluloid belongs to that history, of which we are now becoming so aware, and about which some of us are also becoming quite anxious. Then there's another agenda, reflected in Tom Gunning's remarks, the film-historical one, corresponding to a shift in our attention as film scholars from the film as text and textual object to the film in performance. There too, colour is only one of a range of issues that concern us: sound or musical accompaniment, the role of the lecturer, and so on. This agenda situates colour in the context of our awareness that film in performance is a composite experience of which the film text is only one element - a half-finished product, to use a familiar phrase - which is only completed in performance. Colour thus enters into the whole debate about what film and performance is or might have been.

The third agenda, introduced by Eric de Kuyper, is effectively ideological. At what point, for what reasons, was the awareness of colour suppressed? And we really must talk about it being suppressed. It is a historical-ideological question and has a lot to do with creating a specific cultural place for film, moving it upmarket in fact. Then Ansje van Beusekom's point about the purity of the image becomes an ideological question as much as a physical criterion. It reminds me of the debate in art history about Romanesque churches. People might hate to see them in colour, but they were in fact coloured. It raises those enormous issues of the historical transmission of knowledge in an environment which is always ideological.

Enno Patalas: The issue is not so much restoration or preservation, since we cannot strictly speaking preserve or restore a film. We can't preserve the film material as we can more or less preserve a painting. Furthermore, a film is really something that only exists in a theatre, in the minds of audiences. A present-day audience confronting a tinted and toned film has an entirely different theatrical, cinematic experience than the original audience. In the reviews of the twenties colour is rarely mentioned at all. Films were received, even when tinted and toned, as black-and-white reproductions. When reviewers talked about colour they were talking about the so-called natural colours that were eventually reproduced with new procedures like Technicolor and so on. But it is very rare to find any reflections on tinting and toning during that period.

As for Jacques Ledoux, he thought of silent film as black-and-white because he grew up, like my generation, with black-and-white prints. Colour only came later. It's the same with live-music accompaniment. Eric Rohmer, for instance, is still very much against it, because 'silent' films, in his time, were shown silently. A film is something that happens in your mind, it is not some particular physical thing that remains forever identical, but something that changes over time. It has to be reproduced each time and with each reproduction it is a different film. For each performance, each screening of a film produces a different film. Of course we have to study the old techniques, we have to try and reanimate the old techniques; but what is most important is to be conscious that we are now reproducing the films for a contemporary audience, which is bound to experience them differently from earlier audiences. We often don't know the history of the film material, we often have only parts of the film. How should we show it: with intertitles, explanatory intertitles, and adding colours that have disappeared? I don't in fact think that this is a 'non-historical' point of view. On the contrary, it's a historical question, because history is not something that happened in the past which we can try and reproduce, but rather the past as it is reflected in our minds. It is important to be conscious of this at every step of our work.

Frank Kessler: That critics saw films as black-and-white even when they were tinted and toned has something to do with the fact that if you look at early film theory, the absence of colour, and the absence of sound, were seen as specific aesthetic qualities of cinema. The film aesthetics that you find in books by Munsterberg and Arnheim is built on this difference from reality, which is coloured, and has sounds. There's an ideological aspect, of raising cinema to an art, an art based on silent black-and-white images.

Nico de Klerk: That colour wasn't mentioned in contemporary reviews does not necessarily mean colour wasn't considered important; perhaps the theme was suppressed because the discourse or ideology of the contemporary reviews was different. For instance, there was still some sense that cinema had to be defended, or distinguished from theatre, and in that perspective the colour was not an essential characteristic. The contemporary reviews were mostly about the acting and the mise-en-scène.

If there really was any conscious choice between black-and-white and colour, then among the films we have just seen, there are perhaps one or two where you might speculate that they were specifically made for colour - like DAMNED BE WAR, for example and maybe THE ALHAMBRA, where the colour really enhances the line and form of the building. Of course very often, colour wasn't considered when the film being was made, but was simply added in the production companies' buildings, more with an eye to exhibition, when the colour does become important. Judging from JOKES OF THE JESTERS it may not have been very important what the colours were, as long as there were colours. It's a bit like gift-wrapping in fact, just an extra. That brings me back to what Mark-Paul Meyer said about using your own appreciation in restoring colours. In a sense that is very authentic, because that was sometimes precisely how the exhibitors or distributors worked with these prints - just 'doing something' with them, sometimes even making compilations from different films with colours which may not really have matched but looked nice. Why not do the same with restoration?

Nicholas Hiley: On a general point - it's slightly wrong and maybe we've been misled by Walter Benjamin to think that we are dealing here with two forms of text - the original, as it once existed, as it was created, and the surviving copy. In fact we're dealing with three forms of text: the original which was created in the first thirty years of film, the surviving copy which bears evidence of how it has been handled as well as 'evidence' of how the film was originally made, and then what we are actually arguing about here, a third form, a restoration for modern tastes. Now people have tended to assume that the taste we're discussing here is one of colour, but it isn't, it's historical taste. The taste we want in the prints we're creating from the archival copies is a whole range of tastes, of personal tastes, including a sense of technical accuracy, a historical taste. What we want to see in the copies we produce from the archival originals is something that will satisfy our historical taste, which happens to bend towards a fidelity to the technical processes and the physical appearance of the original. We're not arguing about how to put colour back into films, but how to make coloured films fit our historical taste. I'm not ashamed to have a personal involvement in the creation of new prints, and we are all here because of our tastes; our personal tastes have led us to be interested in silent film. Nobody was ordered to come here, we are here because of our personal emotional involvement. And the level of restoration that we carry out will reflect our own sense of history. It won't be an exact recreation of the original, because none of us want bad projection and bad music, we don't want scratched prints and talking audiences, we don't want to go back to that; we want to create something which satisfies our needs, as historians approaching a period that interests us. And I would argue for the preservation of archival copies, so that the next generation of film historians can make their own choice, according to their tastes. I make decisions about colouring to satisfy my own sense of history, but that doesn't worry me.

Mark-Paul Meyer: Working in the archive, I'm constantly aware that what I'm doing is very personal - in fact, subjective. It's very important to exchange ideas and discuss policies with colleagues from other archives, and with people from other *métiers*. But I'm still the person sitting at the Moviola or the Steenbeck making decisions, deciding about the future of a film. Preserving the original nitrate prints for the next generation is one of the really big worries, because in many archives the nitrate prints, even today, are still being destroyed. Since we're never completely content with our own preservations and aware of the possibilities of the future, it's absolutely imperative to preserve the nitrate prints as long as possible.

William Uricchio: Seeing the colour systems next to one another, what's striking is the breadth of colour systems, the breadth of colour effects, the range of uses to which colour is put over an extended period. Having a very impressionistic feeling for this, I wondered about a couple of things. I'm curious about the range of colour effects we've seen - a range of technical systems and visual effects that cover a relatively long period during which, within many national cinemas, there's a standardisation of certain dramatic forms, certain camera techniques, yet so many variations in colouring. Giovanna Fossati, have you found patterns in this, patterns differentiating genres, patterns differentiating particular producers - Pathé versus Vitagraph, say - patterns across time, say 1912 versus 1922?

Giovanna Fossati: From what I've seen in the archive here, I'd say that with stencilling there are patterns within production companies. There's a difference between Gaumont stencilling and Pathé stencilling. But I haven't really noticed any characteristic patterns in tinting and toning.

Daan Hertogs: As for patterns over time, with fiction films, I wondered whether narrativity becomes so strong in the twenties that the range of colour effects common in the teens just cannot be used anymore. I discovered in a manual that in the twenties a lot of films were printed on pre-coloured stock. Only about twelve colours were available, although that doesn't prevent you from using blue for a love scene, but somehow the limited number of colours shows that conventions were stricter than in the teens.

Peter Delpeut: Watching these coloured silent nitrate prints over four or five years in the archive, my very disturbing experience was that I could find no recipe, no hidden theory, no codes that applied to all the films I saw. This was very disturbing because we're always looking for logic, for codes, but I simply couldn't find any. Every film is a new experience and any code you find in one film is broken in the next. This is what we found in the archive and this is why colour poses such a big problem. Because when you're working through all these films it would be so nice to have recipes and codes to fall back on when you have to make decisions.

Noël Desmet: I worked with Jacques Ledoux for the last 23 years of his life. In 1976 he asked me to find a way of preserving colour, but he was really very severe in his demands. He wanted a new method, because he had no faith in the colour stock whose colours will eventually fade. He also wanted a result that was as close as possible to the original, that would last longer than colour stock, and given the resources of our archive, it had to be cheap. I did a lot of research but only in the last two years of his life did he begin to say I was making progress, getting close, though he still was not satisfied. He did care about colour, even if he said otherwise.

Nicola Mazzanti: In the archives and in the labs, where we decide about the colours, as Peter Delpeut once said, 'we are editing film history'. This is absolutely true, and I always keep this in mind as I work on preserving films. We are actually editing film history, we are doing a job which will influence the future. And this is very tempting and dangerous ground when you're working with colour. Colour in the silents, but also in the sound era, is completely unstable ground. Colour is 'unstable' from the very beginning, because the aesthetics on which colour in the silents is based, is a complicated mix of factors reflecting production, distribution, audience appeal, and sometimes even some colour theory that must have been somewhere in a director's head, for him to leave precise colour plans for a film. We have several examples of very precise colour plans, not just mentioning green, say, but 'green number five', or colouring the intertitles to match the preceding or succeeding scene. Colours were sometimes changed for distribution in other countries - some Italian and French films were given a different set of colours for exhibition in England. So there must have been someone whose job it was to choose the right colours for England. For distribution in a peripheral country or market, you'd have a different set of colours; toning and stencilling would be replaced by simple tinting. Actually, tinting a film is still, like toning, a hell of a job. At the end of the day you're completely yellow, or blue, or green; it's expensive, and the aniline dyes are poisonous. So you need a very good reason to colour a silent film, you didn't just do it because you liked the colours.

Colours are literally unstable, too. In the NFM print of THE LONEDALE OPERA-TOR the blue is stronger at the left and right margins simply because the light of the projector has faded the colour in the centre of the nitrate print. And in a tinted film the colour at the beginning of a 300-metre reel is usually different from the colour at the end. There was just no way of getting the colour even right through the film. I'm not talking about fading here, but simply noting that after you've tinted 5,000 feet of film in one dye bath, and edited a reel, then a shot from an early phase of the colouring process may end up beside a shot from the end of the process, and they will be a different colour.

Then there are the problems of restoration associated with Peter Delpeut's remark that we can never find the code, or rather, that there is no code, or there are hundreds of different codes or patterns for melodrama, for documentary, and so on. Some production companies definitely did follow patterns - Film d'Arte Italiana stencilled more or less systematically, as did Pathé, for some genres, but more work has to be done on this.

We have to preserve what we have now, and very often we don't know exactly what this is, just how faded a certain colour is, say. If we see from the margins that the blue in THE LONEDALE OPERATOR was a certain shade, then we have to restore that blue to the faded centre of the image too. If there's evidence that one particular shot was in black-and-white, then we have to print it in black-and-white. If we can reproduce tinting and toning differently, then we have to do that. In STRAIGHT SHOOTING[2] for instance, there's just one toning, but if you lose it you lose the film. It's in the shot where Harry Carey changes his mind, crying at the graveside, and turns into a good guy. This is emphasized by the toning, it's the only toned shot in the whole film. Make it tinted, or make the rest toned, and he'll remain a bad guy right through the film.

2. STRAIGHT SHOOTING United States (Universal) 1917 Dir. John Ford

SESSION 2:
A Colourful Education

Film programme:

exerpt from: SUNSHINE / *idem* / - ❖ Italy (Incom) Dir. Luciano Emmer ❖ D975 - 281m ❖ Technicolor

AMALFIE / AMALFI / *idem* ❖ Italy (Cines) 1910 ❖ DK926 - 73m / video 144 - 4' tinting, stencil

OP HET MEER VAN LÉMAN / ON LAKE GENEVA / SUR LE LAC LÉMAN ❖ France (Radios) 1913 ❖ DK1200 - 68m (original print length 119m) / video 135 - 4' toning, tinting + toning

LE LAC MAJEUR / LAKE MAGGIORE / [LA SUISSE MERVEILLEUSE] ❖ France (Eclair) 1913 ❖ DK1962 - 70m [original print length 142m] / video 372 - 4' ❖ stencil

THE GLORIOUS WEST COUNTRY / *idem* / *idem* ❖ Great-Britain (Holland America Line) [1925] ❖ DK959 - 349m ❖ stencil

LE ROI DES DOLLARS / THE DOLLAR KING / LE ROI DES DOLLARS ❖ France (Pathé) 1905 Dir. Segundo de Chomón ❖ DK1917 - 34m (original print length 35m) / video 297 - 2' ❖ [hand painting or stencil]

AFSTANDEN 3 / DISTANCES 3 / AFSTANDEN 3 ❖ The Netherlands (Annette Apon Produkties) 1988 Dir. Annette Apon ❖ GZ544-III - 272m ❖ colour stock

EEN AUTOTOCHT IN DE PYRENEEEN / A CAR TRIP IN THE PYRENEES / - ❖ France (Pathé) [1912] ❖ DK276 - 120m / video 324 - 6' ❖ stencil

VALSE TRISTE / *idem* / VALSE TRISTE ❖ United States of America, 1977 Dir. Bruce Conner ❖ FK786 - 59m ❖ tinting

BEGONE DULL CARE / *idem* / BEGONE DULL CARE ❖ Canada 1949 Dir. Norman McLaren ❖ D914 - 212m ❖ hand painting

FLICKER FILM (unfinished) ❖ Canada, 1961 dir. Norman McLaren ❖ black-and-white ❖ print: National Film Board of Canada

exerpt from: CREATIVE PROCESS: NORMAN MCLAREN ❖ Canada (National Film Board of Canada) 1990 Dir. Don McWilliams ❖ print: National Film Board of Canada

ONZE FILMSTERREN / OUR FILM STARS / - ❖ United States of America [1919] DK333 - 220m / video 299 - 11' ❖ tinting

AIDA / *idem* / *idem* ❖ Italy (Film d'Arte Italiana) 1911 ❖ DK1465 - 323m / video 269 - 16' ❖ stencil

ASSEPOESTER / CINDERELLA / CENDRILLON ❖ France (Pathé) 1912 Dir. Ferdinand Zecca ❖ DK223 - 221m (original print length 295m) / video 113 - 12' ❖ tinting, stencil

SCHOOLKAMERADEN / SCHOOL PALS / *idem* ❖ United States of America (Fox) 1923/4 Dir. Lou Seiler, Clyde Carruth ❖ DK391 - 455m / video 079 - 23' black-and-white ❖ contains fragment of:
 - / TWO CHILDREN IN THE WOODS / DEUX ENFANTS DANS LA FORET ❖ France (Pathé) 1912 Dir. Albert Capellani ❖ 210m ❖ stencil

EINE KURIOSE GENERALVERSAMMLUNG / A CURIOUS GENERAL MEETING / [EINE KURIOSE GENERALVERSAMMLUNG] ❖ [Germany (Messter) 1915] ❖ DK596 - 162m / video 075 - 8' ❖ tinting, toning, tinting + toning

Moderator **Don McWilliams**: I'm an independent filmmaker from Canada, and like many other filmmakers, I work a lot with old footage. I'm attracted not so much by the material itself, as by the ways you can use it - to illustrate a point, say. But in the film I'm doing now - a kind of a meditation on what it has been like to live in the twentieth century, made of found footage, found photographs, all that kind of thing - for the first time I've actually been looking at all this old footage for its own sake. There was a lot of discussion in Session 1 about the problem of decay in film, but I'm one of those few filmmakers like Bruce Conner for whom the excitement lies precisely in the decay, the fugitive nature of these images. I find it extremely moving to work with imagery that's mortal. It's moving or exciting to re-use images which are damaged or decaying. For me it's important how sometimes the context, or the reason for it being shot, has disappeared: about fifteen years ago I found some footage from a documentary about World War I made in the early thirties, of a boy, a young man and some women all embracing each other. In my current film I've turned it into a farewell through the type of sound I've used with it. I could easily have found out what it really was, but there's something in the footage itself which transcends its original context.

Something similar happens in the final scene of CREATIVE PROCESS, where I very consciously wanted to recreate in moving images Etienne-Jules Marey's experiments in Paris in the late 1880s. I shot a dancing Norman McLaren twice in black-and-white, first at one frame per second and then at one frame every two seconds. That footage, which is consequently very quick, I manipulated on the optical camera, through mixes of many different speeds. One of the themes of the film is the narcissism of art and artistic creation, so I suddenly decided one day that Norman should dance with himself. So I flipped the film around, giving it 100% exposure on each side of the frame. Where his body overlaps itself, you get a 200%

exposure, and by sheer chance I found - and this relates to this whole business of colouring and toning - you then get a third moving form. Since I was working with colour stock, I was now getting a brown or blue form. Then with grading we were able to get any colour we liked in the overlap. There's all this debate about printing preservations on colour stock, and I had managed, accidentally, to sort of use that problem, and create a kind of a third figure. And this made me realize that we're all part of some sort of tradition.

The film SUNSHINE has all the things that people are supposed to want in cinema: colour, sound, movement. Seeing sunshine in Technicolor made me wonder about the intent behind these various colouring systems. One very obvious function is to provide a kind of helpful cue for the viewer. I mean, they very deliberately made night scenes blue so people would know it was night. It's just there to help move along the action. Also, one dimension of the history of cinema is a constant striving toward naturalism, the attempt to make as real a world as possible. A perfect example of this was FASHION IN MOTION[1] . Someone pointed out to me that it was shot almost as a drama, to make people more interested in these models flitting around. But perhaps it wasn't so much drama as an attempt to make it like real life. And this explains a lot of the adventures into colour. AIDA is a perfect example, which just seems to be crying out for all the wonders of, say, Technicolor and wide-screen. So there's this sort of intent, but there's another, too, which has something to do with the joy of the new art form.

1. Opening screening, Wednesday 26 July: MODE IN BEWEGING / FASHION IN MOTION

You have to ask a basic question here: what is cinema about? For Norman McLaren - and I agree with him - it's about movement. And when you watch these early films of Emile Cohl, Méliès, Segundo de Chomón, people like that, there's also this immense joy in invention for invention's sake. All the wonderful stencilling you see in THE DOLLAR KING for example, is about having fun with colour. Then there's a psychological aspect with colour. What mood does it create, as it breaks all the rules about colour we have today? Although the colour is itself part of the action - a very significant part in some of these early films - it isn't coloured film, it's colour itself playing. There's no theory, it's the birth of an art form, with people experimenting and playing. A film like THE GLORIOUS WEST COUNTRY, a sort of twenties Merchant-Ivory, has one scene that could have been done on modern colour stock. It's a film about nostalgia, which is very clear from the intertitles. It's a kind of England of the mind, but what did the artists who made it, and viewers of that time, think about this film? This also relates to the question Giovanna Fossati addressed, about the differences between the colouring of different companies. You can see clearly enough that each company was aiming at its own distinct colour system. But how did the audiences respond? Did they differentiate? And did they prefer one over the other? It seems clear from watching these films that audiences saw films differently from us. Some of the dramas have a very strange continuity; we see what seem to us basic conventions being disregarded, but did the original audiences notice? Did they become confused, did they care? Then there's the big question about how those audiences watched the film? Were they silent? The cinemas of my childhood certainly weren't. Those are the historical questions I find really interesting.

William Uricchio: You can hardly call Technicolor 'naturalistic', but there does indeed seem to be some sort of movement in colour technologies toward naturalism. In Session 1, I wanted to emphasize the elasticity, the spectrum, of colour techniques and colour sensibilities - which seem pretty strong in this period. In the depiction of nature, the colouring of nature, I see this variation in a remarkably strong way. Gaumont for example, especially in their water and boating shots, impresses by its colour - some of the most naturalistic colour from the period - and even today it's incredible imagery. But in Pathé's A CAR TRIP IN THE PYRENEES there are red and pink stones, and green and blue water, which seem incredibly unnaturalistic. The idea of people having fun with colour is really important.

I came across an article from 1907 about the Niagara Falls. For thirty consecutive nights, the Falls were illuminated in colour. Initially there were fears that this was so garish, so unnatural, that it shouldn't have been allowed. But the press response was quite different. They talk about bringing back the old glory of the Niagara Falls by lighting them in red, yellow and blue - bringing back the natural splendour of the Falls - hiding the ugly factories that had grown up along the sides of the river and bringing back nature. Reports in *The New York Daily Tribune* and *The Post* also talk about the spectacular aspect. I'm really struck by the range of sensibilities: these days a film like A CAR TRIP IN THE PYRENEES might seem spectacular, unnatural, crude compared to Gaumont films of the same period. But if I think about the reception of this Niagara Falls event, then maybe it's emphatically natural, enhances the natural, brings people closer to nature. So this idea of fun and trying to really activate in the period is a compelling one.

Tom Gunning: I know, of course, that Bill Uricchio knows very well that 'nature' is one of those words like 'real' or 'accurate' that we have to be very careful with; they mean very different things in different contexts.

The Niagara Falls example is very interesting, and in some of the travel films there's a feeling that the colour is less an accurate depiction of something, than some sort of energy the thing gives off. It's important to keep this in mind. And since colour still photography remained very expensive in this period, and very unreliable, there's a context of postcards and magic lantern slides with hand-painted images that predated cinema and undoubtedly influenced cinema a great deal. If you look at things like the lantern slides of Burton Holmes or postcards from this period you find a similar range of colour. Another interesting thing is that this sort of colouring was actually controversial. There was a very strong feeling among the cultural elite that mechanically-produced colour, in postcards or chromolithographs and so on, was bound to be false, mainly because it was very garish, very extreme.

And the popularity of these colours among the mass audience had to do less with naturalism as we would normally understand it, than with extremes of emotion almost, or sensuality - a kind of intensity. Very often what gets coloured, for instance in THE GREAT TRAIN ROBBERY[2], is not what is most natural, but what is most extreme. In THE GREAT   2. Session 1

TRAIN ROBBERY there's no colour until suddenly the safe explodes, and the smoke, one of the most evanescent things, gets coloured, the gunshots too. It's important to realize that the colour is very often precisely an effect, rather than a quality of an object: a way of affecting the audience. But at the same time there's an enormous range here: THE GLORIOUS WEST COUNTRY is deliberately very muted, and more accessible to a sort of middle-class taste. Nicholas Hiley emphasized the variety of taste; but tastes don't just vary over time, there are competing tastes, different aspects of taste, at any particular time.

Eric de Kuyper: One theme that has come up here should be stressed: having fun with colours, the pleasure of the cinema. Serge Daney said - though not about colour - something very essential: *Le cinéma c'est l'enfance* - cinema is childhood. Colour also is an aspect of pleasure, of having fun, of childhood - in some periods this is more dominant, in other periods less. In the twenties there's much less fun in feature films, because they were more adult. You get in earlier pictures interesting aspects of colouring and colour-effects, but in features it's almost gone. The pleasure, the sensuality, and the nonsensical dimension of the use of colour is very important. Why is the dress yellow, in the dance-scene in THE GREAT TRAIN ROBBERY? It's not so much the most beautiful woman at the dance, in the group, that you notice, but the yellow of her dress. The other women wear different colours that don't stand out so much. There's this aspect of just playing with the material, and colour is a very interesting ingredient to play with, gives so many possibilities to play with. And it's a nonsensical effect, it has no reason at all. This dimension of colour in film at certain periods should be stressed.

Nico de Klerk: A short question to Eric de Kuyper: would you then say that a story film, or even a nonfiction, is sometimes just an excuse to play with colour?

Eric de Kuyper: Not an excuse - the use of colour, as an addition, is a late intervention in the film's production. Someone - who knows who - chose to make this dress yellow, and that's an addition. It's another dimension, a performance on a text. The film, or rather, this sequence wasn't made for that yellow - not at that time anyway. With Vincente Minnelli certain shots are made for a certain colour, but that didn't happen in the period of tinting, toning and so on. Of course, when there's a fire, it's a sort of pretext to have red. But in general there's a liberty with the material, a kind of free play with the original material, playing around with it, a certain kind of presentation, an addition. As Tom Gunning remarked in Session 1, it's similar to the effect of music on the images, it plays with them, there's an interplay, giving an extra-textual dimension. That's what I like about these colours, about these added, non-photographic colours: they add another dimension to the filmic discourse.

Frank Kessler: Continuing with the problem of the colour-effect, and William Uricchio's point about realism: the two films about lakes in this session - ON LAKE GENEVA then LAKE MAGGIORE - were very interesting. The first was tinted and toned, the second stencilled. The stencilling did convey some realism, but the tinted and toned film was strange because with a travelogue on a lake you'd expect greenish or blueish tinting and toning, rather than the very bright orange-reddish tone we saw, which went in a completely different direction from naturalism.

Very often with stencilling only some parts of the image - especially clothes - are coloured. But even with tinting and toning, which affect the image as a whole, you get the same tendency toward colour effects rather than a naturalistic effect.

Daan Hertogs: Maybe the first film, precisely through its single tone, gives a more or less coherent feeling or tone to the whole content, a journey on a lake, while the stencilled film can be seen as separate shots, as moving postcards. Isn't the colour like a continuous musical score in the first film, but more like disjointed fragments of music accompanying the shots in the second?

Jacques Aumont: Don McWilliams asked about the intent behind the use of colour, the purpose or function of colour. We've heard three answers to his question so far. The first answer turned on pleasure: colour's there because it's pleasing; the second reason suggested was to do with experimentation; the third pointed to ideology - colour embodying tendency toward naturalism, realism, etcetera. I don't quite agree with these answers. As for experimentation, for instance, I definitely disagree with Don McWilliams, because to me experimentation is a very strong word. One experiments when one has a problem to solve. I doubt that the people who made THE GLORIOUS WEST COUNTRY had any problem in mind, any problems with representation. They were simply borrowing the genre of landscape from painters, and reproducing it in film. One might also remark that two of these answers are almost mutually exclusive: how far can you combine experimentation and pleasure? But my basic point is that these three answers and various others that may come up share a common characteristic: they are historical, they are our answers. It's our pleasure we're discussing, rather than the pleasure of spectators in 1910. It's our experimentation, Bruce Conner's, Don McWilliams' experimentation, the experimentation of all the artists who for five or ten years now have been part of the spectacular revival of using found footage, lost footage, stock shots and so on. It's our conception of naturalism, our non-naïve conception of naturalism, because we all know that naturalism, realism, and the rest are big 'isms', ideological movements that we tend to approach as the movement of ideas. In fact we're beginning here to answer the questions of Session 1: why are archives preserving these films in colour? There are these reasons, but there are probably more.

Nicholas Hiley: This joyous use of colour, this sort of revelling in colour, and the elitist attempt to control the mechanical use of colour around the 1890s, 1900s, echo the question of whether there was a class bias in colour over that period - whether colour was so to speak class specific. Was it relatively more expensive to live in a world of colour in the 1890s, 1900s than today? There's some evidence to suggest that the majority of the population lived in a world which wasn't highly coloured, that there was no mass access to the sorts of brightly coloured clothes, paints, inks, dyes, which we now take for granted. Perhaps we should see the colouring of film as a sort of revelling in this scarce resource. Colours in the nineteenth century were very fugitive: think of nineteenth-century drawing rooms, heavily curtained so that colours wouldn't fade. Coloured clothes were expensive, and not very durable. Audiences went to the cinema in their work clothes, in Britain at least; work clothes were not highly coloured, it made no sense for them to be highly coloured. Perhaps colour was used in films not so much to make them necessarily more realistic or artistic, but to make them more luxurious, to provide a world of colour that was otherwise not available. One of the most interesting films here is CONWAY CASTLE[3]: as the train proceeds along the track the fields and the castle are a sort of brown, a roof and a signal are red. But when the train passes through the station, two colours are used for the advertising posters. There's a lot of evidence to suggest that for the majority of the population in the 1890s and 1900s, highly-coloured advertising material was the prevalent source of colour, of bright colour. In pictures of working-class interiors and working-class schools, you very often see advertising posters, advertising images on the walls. Colour had a sort of class specificity, it was actually put there for the audiences that watched these coloured films.

3. Session1

Mariann Lewinsky: Maybe it's gender-specific too: colour as more feminine than black-and-white. Look at the fashion films in the Opening Screening. Fashion, like the colouring of these films, involves not so much a code as choices or options or fun and so on - a whole range of vocabulary that's not very easy to analyse and not very clear as a system. We tend to imagine the colours must form a complete and closed system, but here in fact we have different fields of gravity pulling in different directions, working in different ways. Stencilling in a landscape film accentuates the forms of trees and stones that might otherwise be difficult to discern, but with a dress it enhances the beauty and decoration. And you might contrast the extensive display of dresses in this early period with a greater concentration on faces - where colour is more difficult to apply - in the twenties. This is why these films in the twenties get less colour. The ideological dimension also involves several fields of gravity. Black-and-white is seen as more noble, classic, male, serious, arty, while colour is something arbitrary. It's like clothing the body of the film, where there are lots of different choices. It's hopeless trying to find a code when there are so many interchangeable options.

Daan Hertogs: Do you get different 'fields of gravity' in the same film? That would make them very difficult to analyse, because you'd get changes of direction, even in a single shot.

William Uricchio: These fields of gravity - in other words, a kind of instability in the functioning, in the meaning of colour - can be very productively approached by considering the context that Nicholas Hiley described. What is the place of

AMALFI (Session 2) *nitrate*

SUNSHINE (Session 2) *acetate*

THE GREAT TRAIN ROBBERY (Session 1) *acetate*

DE STAALFABRIEKEN KRUPP (Session 3) *nitrate*

colour in that wider world? Was it actually a black-and-white world? In New York, for example, signs using electric light, which were vividly coloured, first appear around 1891; by 1910 one of New York's attractions is a Roman chariot in moving coloured lights. In Session 1 Frank Kessler mentioned the opposition to colour among of a lot of film theorists - especially a theorist like Arnheim working in the twenties. The breakthrough for mass-produced colour products - at least in the US, but probably in the West as a whole - came in the mid twenties. That's the period when coloured laquer paints for cars finally become available. General Motors produces a red car in 1925, Parker begins making red pens rather than just black ones, towel manufacturers start making coloured towels rather than just white ones, tile manufacturers start using colours, basement furnaces go from black to blue sometime in the late twenties. Around 1925, the development of printing technology allows advertising to be done cheaply in colour. With other manufacturing breakthroughs, colour is now available to the masses in consumer products. I wonder if that advent of colour coincides with the maturity or the adulthood of films, in Eric de Kuyper's phrase - the use of colour as a kind of an adult conceit. And the critics, at the point where colour becomes generally available in the culture, retreat with film, saying that film should be black-and-white because that is the defining artistic feature of the medium. Is there some perverse inverse relationship between the availability of consumer goods in colour and film's own definition of colour as pure fun, producing a retreat to black-and-white?

Tom Gunning: In the United States - though Europe may be a little different - the domain of colour is in effect being claimed around the turn of the century by the lower middle class and to some extent by the working class. This is very upsetting for the upper classes. They feel that they should control colour, because they understand it as a rarity, as the product of craftsmanship. They know there's a great difference between a carefully executed oil-painting and a mechanically reproduced chromolithograph. They're worried about colour becoming too widely available and losing its subtlety and grace. It's interesting how around the turn of the century very bright, garish colours become more and more associated with the working class and the lower middle class. In fact it becomes an issue of class taste - the middle class, the upper middle class and the upper class begin to be more restrained in their use of colour. Colour becomes very much associated with the kind of downmarket advertising that Nicholas Hiley mentioned, with popular art, vaudeville, circus, carnival - it becomes the lowest common denominator of vulgar taste. But when we start talking about mass production, about automobiles and designer towels and so on, this is definitely a middle-class rather than a working-class phenomenon. In the twenties, the upper middle classes are in some sense prepared to share the pleasures that had been frowned upon by the elite. This is also the period, in the twenties, when motion pictures are totally embraced by the middle class and begin to take the middle classes and their consumer pleasures as their main topic. Actually, in the early years of cinema and the teens, we see a very interesting in-between phase where colour's being wrested away from the cultural elite. It was also being redefined in a very bright and garish way, although still somewhat different from the way that it would be generally adopted by the consumer society in the twenties, when it was colour-coordinated and toned down. The colours of the towels and cars of the twenties are in fact like the colours in THE GLORIOUS WEST COUNTRY, muted pastel tones very different from something like the Pathé 's A CAR TRIP IN THE PYRENEES.

Stephen Bottomore: We've discussed several motives for colour in films: pleasure, experiment, realism, luxury and so forth. I wonder if there's another factor which might play some part - especially in the stencilled or hand-coloured films - which is purely functional. I mean, the use of colour to clarify narrative, parallel to other practices with a similar aim in the period before about 1910. If you have a wide shot, and obviously a lot of films at this time were done in wide shots, you have small figures in the frame, so how do you draw attention to the action that is taking place somewhere in the frame? There were in fact a large number of strategies. First of all, a commentator, who could point out things taking place in the picture. Slightly later on, another strategy would be cutting in to a closer shot, so people can clearly see what's happening, see the action. You might see the use of stencilled colour as a kind of halfway house to seam the section. If you have certain important figures, doing important things in the frame, you might colour the figure as precisely as you can, as one way of drawing the attention of the viewer to that part of the frame.

Hans-Michael Bock: We've been jumping back and forth from one side of the screen to the other. The pleasure and enjoyment is on the audience side. The experimentation with film is on the filmmaking side. But we haven't really considered the people who actually decided to colour the films and how to do this: in the early period it was the sales people. In the teens films were sold as black-and-white or coloured; colour added a special attraction, a kind of selling-point. Later on, colour was added without this being mentioned in advertisements or elsewhere. So as a selling-point it seems by then to have disappeared, or to be taken for granted. Whether films should be coloured or left black-and-white had by then become an artistic decision.

Carlos Bustamante: Stephen Bottomore made a good point, because colour makes things visible, it marks the presence of things. In Gorki's first reactions to the first films, he talks about the tones of grey, comparing them with ghosts. None of us could have thought of ghosts, watching the films in Session 1 and 2. As Tom Gunning said of the explosions, for example, colour makes it an attraction, draws your attention to them.

Sabine Lenk: Getting back to pleasure - if I came from a commercial archive I'd want to find out what people like today because in the teens and twenties colour was a commercial factor, it helped sell films because people were attracted by the colour. Maybe historians, like myself, from noncommercial archives, should keep this in mind a little as we try to recreate what we call a near-original copy. Also, from a historical point of view, I wonder why we find so few articles on the effect of colour on those early audiences. Most of what we find written about colour is the technical stuff in the manuals about getting as close as possible to the 'natural' colours of nature. In the nontechnical trade press they're usually complaining that colours aren't close enough to nature.

Richard Abel: One kind of pleasure - the producer's pleasure - is the pleasure of capital, of acquiring capital. During their first decade or two in cinema Pathé developed the stencil colouring system as one of their main products. Their films were a way of displaying their stencil process and they were extremely effective in exploiting this in the United States. If you read the trade press, whenever colour-ed films are mentioned between 1905 or 1906 until around 1910, they're always associated with Pathé. Pathé was known as the company that produced coloured films, and we shouldn't overlook their pleasure in acquiring capital by exploiting colour.

Coby Bordewijk: If you look at the advertisements for those early films made for uneducated people - for the lower classes - shown in very simple cinemas, you can see that the real function of colour was to make money. It was 'kitsch' for the lower classes, who were thrilled to see colour in their lives. We have tranformed their pleasure in kitsch into our pleasure in camp. Our enjoyment of these colours is a kind of meta-enjoyment.

Don McWilliams: We're currently living in a period where we are driven by technology in film, and if you don't adapt your work to these technologies, you're considered very old-fashioned. How do questions of technology relate to all the ways colour was developed and used in the early period? I'm hearing all sorts of arguments here about why the films were coloured, but how far was tech-nology, rather than people wanting to use particular techniques or find particular ends, driving developments in the colour systems? Was stencilling, for instance, developed as a response to public demand for more realistic colour, or simply because somebody realized they could have machine stencilling and make very colourful films and make lots of money?

Ine van Dooren: The key thing is that most of these films were coloured to make money, and it was the production companies who added the colour. There was a long history of using colour before it was used in cinema - colour in post-cards, in chromolithographic prints, in magic lantern slides - of which all sorts of people, including people in film production companies, were well aware. Colour didn't just 'come up' in the teens, all the systems of colouring were already there.

Sabine Lenk: The discussion about the pleasure of seeing colours made me think of De Mille - one of the greatest filmmakers because of the colours he chose. But I've read that he said people shouldn't pay attention to the colours he put in his films but to the story. The story was the important thing. This is strange because he developed, with Wiekov and Handschiegel, his own colour process. The nitrate prints in the George Eastman house have twenty or twenty-five different colours in the tinting and toning.

Richard Abel: Paolo Cherchi Usai says that in his research in archives he's found very few American films before 1910 that use colour of any kind. Given the importance of a commercial aesthetic of colour and light, particularly in the United States, but probably in Europe too, why is it that a company like Pathé exploited coloured films in the United States, yet American companies didn't exploit colour? Why do American films tend not to be released in colour until 1909 or 1910?

Peter Delpeut: I was surprised, knowing what Paolo Cherchi Usai has said, when we got the beautifully coloured print of THE GREAT TRAIN ROBBERY that was shown in the first session, from the United States. It seems to suggest that colour prints were a normal thing in this period.

Three short closing remarks: first, the discussion so far has tended not to differentiate between monochrome tinting and toning on the one hand, and stencilling and hand-colouring on the other. But they're two completely different systems with two completely different problems, or patterns of problems. We should make a clear distinction between them.

Secondly, we should be more careful to distinguish between the way the films were experienced when they were first shown and our experiences now. Otherwise we will mix up all kind of things.

My last remark is that the audiences of these early films must actually have been quite intelligent to be able to understand all the different meanings involved in the use of colours.

A Slippery Topic:
Colour as Metaphor, Intention or Attraction?

Film programme:

DE PETROLEUMBRAND TE VLISSINGEN. EEN OVERZICHT VAN DE RUINE / PETROLEUM
FIRE AT FLUSHING. A VIEW OF THE RUINS / - ❖ The Netherlands (Pathé) [1917]
DK1343 - 11m / video 153 - 1' ❖ tinting

exerpt from: DE STAALFABRIEKEN KRUPP / THE KRUPP STEEL WORKS / - ❖ Germany
(Friedrich Krupp AG) [1916] ❖ DK1092 - 366m / video 069 - 8' ❖ tinting

DE KONING DER BANDIETEN OF HET GEHEIM DER CATACOMBEN / THE KING OF BAN-
DITS OR THE SECRET OF THE CATACOMBS / [ZIGOMAR] ❖ France (Eclair) 1911 Dir.
Victorin Jasset ❖ DK1218 - 259m / video 135 - 13' ❖ tinting, toning

BITS & PIECES NO.73 / *idem* / - ❖ [Germany or United States of America, 1915]
DK914 - 40m / video 009 - 2' ❖ tinting

PARK UND GROSSE WASSER VON VERSAILLES / THE PARK AND THE GREAT FOUNTAIN
AT VERSAILLES / LES GRANDES EAUX DE VERSAILLES ❖ France (Pathé) [1904]
DK318 - 38m / video 062 - 2' ❖ hand painting

STORM OP ZEE / STORM AT SEA / [TEMPETE DANS LE GOLFE DE GASCOGNE]
France (Gaumont) [1910] ❖ DK659 - 43m [original print length 53m] / video
027 - 2' ❖ tinting, toning + tinting

EEN BOOTTOCHT LANGS DE WATEREN VAN DE ARDECHE / A BOAT TRIP ON THE
WATERS OF THE ARDECHE / [DESCENTE EN BARQUE À TRAVERS LES GORGES DE
L'ARDECHE] ❖ France (Gaumont) [1910] ❖ DK525 - 62m [original print length
131m] / video 027 - 3' ❖ stencil, tinting + stencil

UITSTAPJE DOOR HET DAL VAN DE TARN, VAN SAINT-ÉNIMIE NAAR ROZIER / A TRIP
THROUGH THE VALLEY OF THE TARN, FROM SAINT-ÉNIMIE TO ROZIER / LES GORGES
DU TARN ❖ France (Gaumont) [1911] ❖ D3980 - 139m (original print length 132m) /
video 052 - 6' ❖ black-and-white

DE PESCARA / THE PESCARA / IL PESCARA ❖ Italy (Ambrosio) 1912 ❖ DK93 - 77m
(original print length 107m) / video 144 - 4' ❖ tinting

NAT PINKERTON / *idem* / *idem* ❖ France (Eclipse) 1911 ❖ Dir. Pierre Bressol
DK375 - 200m / video 105 - 10' ❖ tinting

MOOI ZWITSERLAND / BEAUTIFUL SWITZERLAND / [LA SUISSE MERVEILLEUSE]
France (Eclair) 1913 ❖ DK301 - 70m [original print length 142m] / video 062 - 4'
toning, stencil, toning + stencil

BLOEMENVELDEN HAARLEM / FLOWER FIELDS, HAARLEM / - ❖ The Netherlands
[(F.A. Nöggerath or Alberts Frères) 1909] ❖ DK686 - 32m ❖ hand painting or
stencil

BLOEMENWEELDE / A WEALTH OF FLOWERS / - ❖ France (Gaumont among others)
[1914] ❖ DK1433 - 27m / video 224 - 2' ❖ hand painting, stencil

exerpt from: VAN BOL TOT BLOEM / FROM BULB TO FLOWER / VAN BOL TOT BLOEM
The Netherlands (Multifilm) 1931 Dir. J.C. Mol ❖ DK1677 - 1367m (original print
length 1488m) / video 266 - 66' ❖ tinting

LEER OM LEER / TIT FOR TAT / LA PEINE DU TALION ❖ France (Pathé) 1906 Dir.
Gaston Velle ❖ DK917 - 50m (original print length 100m) / video 113 - 3'
stencil

METAMORPHOSE / METAMORPHOSIS / MÉTAMORPHOSE ❖ France (Pathé) [1905]
D4951 - 65m / video 188 - 4' ❖ black-and-white

TUINENVORSTIN / GARDEN PRINCESS / - ❖ [France (Pathé) 1927] ❖ DK1432 - 84m /
video 224 - 4' ❖ stencil

PARIJSCHE DANCEUSES / PARIS DANCERS / MOULIN ROUGE DANCERS ❖ United
States of America (American Mutoscope & Biograph) [1898] ❖ D5812-XI - 11m
hand painting

exerpt from: BACCHANAAL DES DOODS / BACCHANAL OF DEATH / BACCHANAL DES
TODES ODER DAS OPFER EINER GROSSEN LIEBE ❖ Germany (Central Film Vertrieb)
1917 Dir. Richard Eichberg ❖ DK424 - 734m (original print length 1500m) / video
017 - 36' ❖ toning + tinting

BITS & PIECES NO.278 / idem / - ❖ [France, (Pathé] 1905] ❖ DK1919 - 60m / video
309 - 3' ❖ toning, tinting, toning + tinting

LITTLE TICH, BEROEMDE ENGELSCHE KOMIEK / LITTLE TICH, FAMOUS ENGLISH
COMEDIAN / LITTLE TICH ❖ France (Pathé) 1906-1907 ❖ D5287 - 135m (original
print length 135m) / video 254 - 7' ❖ black-and-white

Moderator **Tom Gunning**: I want to address a series of very specific histori-cal questions - or rather, research problems. But theory and history are inseparable and we can't in fact talk about colour historically without thinking about it theoretically.

After coming here in May for the pre-screenings of these films, I left with a sense of both misery and exaltation. The misery was what one might call the misery of colour, particularly in silent film: I mean its fragility, its vulnerability, all the problems Giovanna Fossati addressed in Session 1, not just colour preservation problems, but the problems of looking at colour, trying to figure out what it was originally, as we look at preservation prints that more or less - often the latter - reflect the original nitrate material. Colour is in many respects one of the most tenuous things we can investigate, and that can be rather depressing. Interwoven with this is that I came to the pre-screenings having seen a lot of silent films, and feeling I more or less knew how colour operated in them. Although the screen-ings didn't totally contradict everything I thought I knew, they certainly shook up many of my assumptions, and I suddenly realized that the role of colour in silent film was a great deal less systematic than I'd thought.

If all these things initially depressed me, they ultimately cheered me up, not only because I like chaos, but also because they made me think about the nature of colour. The difficulties of discussing colour aren't unrelated to the very nature of colour. One of the things that I want to briefly think about theoretically is the fact that, particularly in the western tradition, colour has always been approached as a secondary quality, as something not part of the essence of things. The debate of course has gone back and forth, ranging from philosophy to art, but the gener-al feeling, going back to Plato, has been that somehow the outline, the form of something is more essentially related to the concept and idea of the thing than colour, which seems to be temporary, secondary, seems to have more to do with instants of time and situations than with the eternally knowable. In fact, part of the joy of colour lies in inverting this model, accepting transience. Colour is in-deed less intellectual, less tangible, less eternal than form. It's always somehow associated with the fugitive and the ephemeral. Nicholas Hiley pointed out to me yesterday something that comes out strongly in the films of this and previous ses-sions - that colour is very often represented by flowers. And this reflects not only the brilliant saturation of colour in flowers, but precisely the fact that it's tempo-rary, that it fades. A brilliant moment rather than something that is constant. Then there's the association with fashion, reflected in the first day's screenings, and with clothing. Here, as Frank Kessler pointed out, the colour is associated with something external, ephemeral, inconstant. It's in this sense closely associated with a modern sensibility that, as Baudelaire said, is particularly attuned to things that pass. And cinema of course partakes very strongly in this sensibility. The very way that colour seems to shimmer on top of things with stencilling and hand colouring has this kind of weird insubstantial quality, is part of its joy in the silent era.

Conversely, though, there has always been an attempt to tie colour to certain meanings, associated with the theory that there's some deep essential connection between certain colours and certain emotions. But as Jacques Aumont's study has shown, these associations, although they have certain consistencies, have many inconsistencies, too. We have to see them as cultural constructions whereby colour is associated with certain things while not absolutely tied to them. This is what we find in silent film. There are certain associations, particularly with mono- chrome tints, the most obvious being blue for night, red for fire, or sometimes strong yellow for interior lighting. But what we find as we watch more and more monochrome tinting is that, as Peter Delpeut remarked in Session 1, the codes begin to break down. A couple of people have asked me why we chose NAT PIN- KERTON. One reason is that to some extent it uses the blue-for-night code, but at certain points this is totally contradicted. As Nat Pinkerton sets out to meet the bandits, the film's tinted gold. Presumably he doesn't walk for hours till nightfall, but when he gets there it's blue, and you know the meeting is taking place at night, but then the earlier shot seems oddly tinted. In many of these films, if we watch them carefully, the codes are not consistent. I'm not saying the codes aren't there, but particularly in this period there's a fair amount of free variation along with the codes. This free variation is extremely important; there are codes in this period, there are associations, but they aren't absolutely rigid and are often, in fact, applied in very surprising ways. The codes are in a great deal of flux, and this isn't just something to be decried or ignored, but the key to colour.

We talk about the narrative role of colour, but we very rarely understand what is happening because of the colour. We more often get the meaning of the colour from the narrative situation. The colour can heighten or underscore what's hap- pening in the story at some point, but very rarely creates it. Its role constitues an independent narrative element. Now this is one way of channelling colour toward a certain type of meaning. This aspect of intensity relates to the 'primary' quality of colour, which is precisely its intensity, the way it produces a greater emotional or sensual response. This is one of the ways filmmakers can directly contact the audience and influence them: there are all sorts of variants , but the key thing is a kind of intense sensual communication.

One way to think about this, given its enormous range from intensifying a dra- matic moment to just the pure play of pleasure, is by comparing it with music, and particularly with the way music was used in the early silent era. Music has been ignored in a lot of film history, because it was felt to be external to the film text. Like colour, it wasn't considered essential - particularly in the silent era, where it might change with every viewing, every performance of a film. But we're increasingly realizing that it was extremely important to the film-going experience. Research that one of my graduate students, Tim Anderson, has been doing, looking at some of the trade-journal comments on film music in around 1909-1910, has uncovered a great deal of controversy about music being played in a way that was totally unrelated to the narrative. A recurring complaint is that the pianist is playing to the audience, instead of playing to the film.

There are strong parallels with the colour in the films we have seen so far: it directly stimulates the audience, but often in a fairly free relation to the film. Sometimes there's a very direct relationship, but sometimes just pure play, free variation; grabbing your attention independently of any obvious code. In some films, of course, there's very little narrative to follow - films of flowers, fountains, fireworks, some of the tourist films and many of the trick films, where the colour seems to function as an attraction, a very direct visual stimulus. It's something to look at, something to surprise you, to amaze you, it doesn't necessarily carry any decodable meaning, any paraphrasable meaning, but is purely a kind of sensuous play. Significantly, perhaps, the earliest use of colour was probably Edison's Kinetoscope films of Annabel doing the skirt dance - an entertainment which not only involves these patterns of billowing cloth, but all kinds of projected light of different colours. For many people - not only vaudeville audiences, popular audiences, but also symbolist poets like Mallarmé - this total play of form and light and colour, whose most famous exponent was Loie Fuller, showed the possibility of an art totally detached from literature, from verbal meanings: just pure form and motion. What colour brings to many of these films is just this sense of colour as a pure attraction, something whose very essence is just to be constantly changing. In other words, colour had an enormous sensual impact in the silent era. We can see it being channelled, and it's very exciting to see how it becomes coded, but there's also a kind of resistance to any absolute coding. The colour very often simply indicates a change in the situation, rather than telling us what that change amounts to.

I'll conclude this rather lengthy introduction with a series of research questions, of issues that we must consider. If we now see colour as an essential part of silent film, that's just the beginning, not some conclusion. If we take the figure that has become almost canonical in the last year or so, of 80% of silent film probably having some kind of colour - we need to investigate this further but I think it's probably pretty accurate - then we have to break that figure down. What, first of all, do we mean by 'silent cinema'? Any historian thinks immediately of the many, many different things covered by that term. Most generally, what role does colour play in the various decades and half-decades of silent cinema? For instance, I very much doubt that the 80% figure holds for the period from 1895 to 1905. I'd like to know about the prevalence of colour in that first decade of cinema and then look at each succeeding decade to see how colour persists or changes. One of the most interesting questions is why it eventually disappeared. The usual explanation, and I'm sure there's something in it, is that tinting interfered with the soundtrack. Howver, this wouldn't completely interfere. So my guess is that in the late twenties tinting was already declining. While emphasizing the presence of colour in the silent era, we also have to explain this decline. There's no obvious reason why 80% of thirties films weren't tinted. But apparently they weren't; there was still some tinting, but it was a minor element. Why? What happened? It would also be very interesting to look at different countries. It's very clear that France, with Pathé, was a centre for colour in film, but what about other countries? Richard Abel's research has indicated that until about 1909 the United States didn't produce the amount of coloured film that, say, Pathé did; and this actually gave Pathé a commercial advantage. What about other countries, particularly smaller countries: did they use colour as much as the French? Soviet cinema, for instance, did it use colour? How much, and how? We know about some of the colour experiments that Eisenstein did with THE BATTLESHIP POTEMKIN and OLD AND NEW[1], but it would be very interesting to know more. And we should break down the 80% figure in terms of genre: did all genres use colour equally? It seems that in farces from before World War I there's relatively little colour. Is this actually true, and what is the explanation if it is? Tourist films and *féerique* films, on the other hand, seem to have a lot of colour.

1. BRONENOSETS POTYOMKIN USSR (Goskino) 1925; STAROE I NOVOE USSR (Sovkino) 1929

It's also very important to make distinctions within colour itself. We have the monochrome systems of tinting and toning, we have the photographic colour of the Gaumont Chronochrome system, Prizma Color and so on, and of course we have stencilling and hand-colouring. It's very interesting to consider colour as a whole, but very important at some point to consider the differences, the relations and specificity. Another question: it's true that colour doesn't seem to provoke much comment in most of the reviews that have been reprinted. But maybe we haven't thoroughly mined the trade journals and other material from the period looking for comments on colour, because film history didn't until very recently pay any attention to colour in silent films. I have the feeling that a lot has been ignored. It's probably very significant that most reviews didn't discuss colour. What the significance is I'm not yet prepared to say, but I *will* say that there's probably a lot of information still to be found in contemporary sources.

Finally, I'd like to make a very brief point relating to some of the issues from the first two sessions. My favourite definition of history comes from an American Shakespearean scholar, Greenblatt, who saw historiography as a desire to speak to the dead. We want, obviously, to know what early audiences felt and thought about colour, how they experienced it. But equally obviously, we can't completely recreate this, it's in some ways very distant. Of course, what we're doing as historians isn't so much attempting to resurrect something that's disappeared, as expressing our desire to forge some link with the dead. Forging that link doesn't relate only to the past, it also relates to the present, and even more perhaps our sense of our future. There's no question that the reason we're rediscovering colour now is, as Nicholas Hiley pointed out, because we're interested in colour right now. That doesn't mean our project isn't historical, it obviously is. It expresses our desire to relate in a new way to an aspect of the past which has been ignored, if not suppressed. It's important to realize that our present day interests will always guide us, but that those interests are partly rooted in the past and partly invested with the future, and aren't merely subjective.

Eric de Kuyper: One thing that can teach us a lot is the use of monochrome tinting and toning in feature films, because there's a very big difference between fiction films before the First World War and after it. Before the war monochrome is used to accentuate narrative discontinuity. In a sequence of six or seven shots within the same narrative idea, each shot is coloured differently to distinguish the first shot from the second, the third, and so on. The key question is why this colouring changed after the war. In the twenties colouring becomes less important because the editing, the language, has changed so much.

The discontinuous language of prewar narrative cinema is particularly stressed by the discontinuous use of colour. And if we consider together these three elements of the cinematic performance - colour, music and image - it's very strange to find image and colour discontinuity with musical continuity; not every shot has a different musical theme. There's some sort of dialectical interplay between the discontinuous image and colour, and the continuity of the music evoking a sort of coherent framework.

Tom Gunning: It's precisely this discontinuity that's so striking, and that seems, in fact, uncoded. It's as though the colouring turns on changes of shot, rather than changes in the story. It's a discontinuity that gets evened out, smoothed out in the twenties, as you said, with editing and the further coding of colour.

Heide Schlüpmann: Up till now we've tended to ask why there's colour in these films. Maybe it would make more sense to ask why later we get black-and-white films, because when you look at early cinema and its precedents in the exhibition context, there was always colour. Look at the magic lantern, the panorama, the variety shows with light-effects and coloured light. Maybe we should first consider the use of colour in these older traditions, because they define the context of early cinema. Watching THE TRIP THROUGH THE VALLEY OF THE TARN... after A BOAT TRIP ON THE WATERS OF THE ARDECHE, I was struck by the black-and-white aesthetic. It was really emphasized by all this colour - it makes a very strong impression after all these coloured films.

In relation to this context, Peter Delpeut asked in Session 2 about the difference between different colour systems. I have the impression that one key difference is the difference between colouring images and colouring light. Brush or stencil colouring seems more to do with colouring images, while tinting and toning have more to do with colouring light.

Mariann Lewinsky: Tom Gunning mentioned temporality and eternity: perhaps we could take this a little further. Watching this session's films I felt very strongly that applied colour has no temporal dimension: it's pure presence. This is true of toning and tinting too, if the colours change frequently - there's only presence. It's also true for changed or faded colours that have nothing to do with the original colour. Whether a film was made three weeks ago or a hundred years ago, we experience the colour now. In a film with fairly long monochrome sequences, and with black-and-white, you have a unity of time in the film. This means that with nonfiction you have a documentary unity, and with fiction you have a unity of diegetic time, the time of the fiction. Watching a black-and-white film nowadays, there's somehow a strong association with memory; with Bruce Conner's monochrome VALSE TRISTE you feel it's outside the present, either memory or fiction. But with changing colours, they're always present now, independent of time. Colour is now, it's a performing art.

Sabine Lenk: I guess, to echo Tom Gunning, that early audiences must have had a very different perception of colour. Gorki's account of his first encounter with film contrasts strongly with the first articles written by journalists in Lyons and Paris. In France they said, OK, the colours are missing, but it's wonderful to see these very vivid images of our life, to see dead members of the family coming back to life - they were delighted. But Gorki was saying that a very important part of life was missing, the essential part, colour. The two films Heide Schlüpmann mentioned, A BOAT TRIP ON THE WATERS OF THE ARDECHE and A TRIP THROUGH THE VALLEY OF THE TARN..., are very good examples of this. The pastel colours of the Ardèche are very vivid, but then we see the depth of the Tarn gorges in black-and-white. I was very struck by the contrast, which exactly reflects what Gorki felt when he saw black-and-white films.

Eric de Kuyper: As for this contrast between colour and black-and-white, one has to accept that colour has something to do with vulgarity, crudeness, childishness, 'popular' taste. Let's add some colour, you say in theatre or fashion - or let's tone it down to avoid bad taste. There really is this tension between good and bad taste. Colour, measured by our cultural codes, is usually on the side of bad taste. Colours are dangerous. But I must mention something I saw last weekend in London. People were going to a royal Garden Party, and I never saw such yellows, such reds, such blues, such greens in my life. They were real colours, and these were distinguished British people going to a royal Garden Party. I'm amazed by our cultural codes of colour.

Péter Forgács: A few questions to Tom Gunning, because I was really struck by his short note about this session in the printed booklet. In his closing sentence he promised to explore some answers, rather than merely pose questions; to 'trace the intentions behind the use of colour in silent film, whether as referents, metaphors, narrative guides, or pure attractions.' We've had quite a few remarks about pure attraction, but I'm curious to hear something about the other factors, in this context of colour as a kind of cultural construction, both then and now. If colour in films was borrowed from colour in still photography, then the intention was not simply to sell colour, but in some sense to sell the still or moving image as something more than an attraction. The colour is a kind of emotional guide, not a purely visual sensation, but also a kind of subconscious feeling in the viewer. You might here talk of references or metaphors or narrative guides as a kind of naive way to influence the viewer's subconscious. Take today's television where you sometimes see some black-and-white footage in, say, music videos or documentaries. This means something, not only because of our association of black-and-white with the past, or with a document or real evidence. I see war reports from Bosnia on television with blood everywhere, but I can be more shocked by black-and-white footage from the Second World War. Maybe if photography, which began in black-and-white, had begun in colour, somebody would have had to invent black-and-white. Our problem, as Thomas Elsaesser said in the first session, is that we ourselves are at a cultural crossroads and are therefore looking back in a new way. I'd like to hear some discussion of this question, which I find particularly interesting.

Tom Gunning: I meant the 'referents' in the teaser to my talk to be an allusion to the idea of accuracy or verisimilitude - the water was blue, so we stencil it blue. Obviously, this is one of the motivations for colouring, for stencil colouring especially. Narrative guides and metaphors are closely associated - take ZIGOMAR, where the explosion is completely red. It's more of a metaphorical red than a referential red, even though explosions might produce fire; with the final explosion, the shot is actually red before the explosion occurs. That may reflect practical questions of colour processing, but it wasn't a problem for filmmakers or audiences because it refers to a kind of emotion associated with the scene. One of the ways that colour becomes channelled over time in silent film, and more generally, is through a growing dichotomy between either recognizing it as making a reference to something in real life, or understanding it as a metaphor for how you're supposed to feel, how you're supposed to respond. What interests me are the limitations of this division, the trouble it gets into. The blue of the water is more blue than any water we've ever seen, so this referent becomes almost a kind of a metaphor. Likewise, the red of the explosion becomes multi-referential, taking in the explosion, the violence, the blood, the death. The confusion between reference and metaphor often produces very strange effects. What are we supposed to make of one of the very first images in THE PESCARA, where the water is shockingly green? Is it a metaphor for something? For what? I find this fascinating because we can't anchor any specific feeling in the image. In THE KRUPP STEEL WORKS, there's an almost uniform reddish, pinkish, or goldenish tint that evokes the overwhelming heat. It turns the film into the best version I've ever seen of Dante's inferno, with this overwhelming metaphor that bleeds into so many different areas.

I'm really interested in the way these things can't be controlled. The colours always resonate with all sorts of meanings and associations, which in the silent era aren't really controlled. For me this defines the use of colour in the early silent era down to, and maybe during, the First World War. It's as though the energy is allowed to expand, as though filmmakers haven't yet decided to contain it, as they later would.

Hans-Michael Bock: Can we return for a moment to the question of black-and-white? After the screening of Eisenstein's THE BATTLESHIP POTEMKIN in Berlin, the press specifically mentioned the red flag at the climax of the film being painted. That suggests not only that the film was shown in black-and-white, but that this was standard by that time - why else would they have paid such attention to the red flag? So the tradition of hand painting must by that time have been forgotten, at least by the reviewers. Another point we should keep in mind is that early in the twenties black-and-white stock changed from orthochromatic material to panchromatic material. In the trade papers you read that technicians had big problems colouring panchromatic material. They discussed how they could do it, but there were problems. Maybe this switch from orthochromatic to panchromatic material as the main print stock changed the use of colour too: colouring must have become more expensive, and maybe this explains why it was dropped?

Enno Patalas: There was always opposition to tinting, at least in Germany, in the twenties but earlier too, among producers and filmmakers. This had to do with a growing awareness in the twenties of the photographic nature of cinema. From the very beginning this conception of the photographic nature of cinema supported the use of black-and-white, and maybe toning, but worked against tinting. Oskar Messter said that tinting had always been there just for the audience. With the growing sophistication or mastery of the photography, tinting became less important.

In Germany, however, most films were tinted till the very end of the twenties. I don't see why the change to panchromatic stock was such a problem, because although panchromatic material had to be used for the negatives, the prints could easily have been done on orthochromatic material. Once the image was on black-and-white stock, you could use orthochromatic material for the prints. But as early as 1920 FROM MORNING TO MIDNIGHT[2] was announced as being in black-and-white and thus true to the photographic nature of cinema. Most films were tinted during the twenties, but there was a whole series of individual films in black-and-white, like DR. MABUSE, THE GAMBLER[3] and Murnau's FAUST[4] and THE LAST LAUGH[5] - films in which the camera-work was becoming more important. And the fact that became it possible to film at night or at dawn meant you didn't need blue-for-night any more, as it did in NOSFERATU[6] where the night sequences with the vampire were meant to be blue. With the growing awareness of the photographic nature of cinema and a growing stress on camera movement and so on, colour became less important. One aspect that needs researching is what the auteurs, the filmmakers, felt about colour? I've been through Murnau's own annotated copies of his scenarios, hoping to find something on colour. All I could find was a point in the scenario for VOGELÖD CASTLE[7] where he notes: 'dream sequences - leave them black-and-white'.

2. VON MORGENS BIS MITTERNACHT Germany (Ilag-Film) 1920 Dir. Karl-Heinz Martin

3. DR. MABUSE, DER SPIELER Germany (Uco-Film) 1922 Dir. Fritz Lang

4. Germany (Ufa) 1926

5. DER LETZTE MANN Germany (Ufa) 1924

6. Germany (Prana-Film) 1921 Dir. Friedrich Wilhelm Murnau

7. SCHLOSS VOGELÖD Germany (Uco-Film) 1921

Daan Hertogs: The technological explanations for the disappearance of colour at the period when sound was introduced aren't completely satisfactory. JOHANN STRAUSS in Session 1 was a tinted sound film. The sound - which heightens the realism - and the colour just don't seem to mix very well. As a 'historical' film it's in some sense non-realistic, and maybe this relates to something I think Ed Buscombe wrote about Technicolor being used in the thirties for non-realistic genres like musicals and fantasies.

Tom Gunning: That whole question about colour versus black-and-white in relation to realism versus non-realism is extremely vexed, because you can go through different periods of film history, and the relation switches around. Murnau's wanting the dream sequences left black-and-white is really fascinating, because you might expect the opposite. But there may be something else at work here. I recently saw THIS IS CINERAMA[8], the original Cinerama film, at Bradford. Cinerama, of course, introduced the wrap-around screen as a visual effect and stereo as a sound effect, and one of the most striking things

8. THIS IS CINERAMA United States (Lowell Thomas Company) 1952

was a sequence where the stereophonic sound is really important. It begins with a shot of empty choir-stalls, then you suddenly hear voices, behind you in fact: the choristers are singing and as they come forward, you see them come in past the camera, and you hear the sound moving forward as they fill up the screen. Now, that sequence is not in Technicolor like the rest of the film, but in sepia, in monochrome. I imagine they wanted to direct the audience's attention to the sound here rather than at the beginning of the film with its roller-coaster and visual razzle-dazzle. They wanted to drain the colour so you'd be more tuned to the sound.

The influence of panchromatic film is very interesting, even if colouring wasn't really a technical problem. With the introduction of panchromatic material, which has a greater range of contrast, you wouldn't want the tint to hide the beauty of this novelty. And with the introduction of sound maybe there's a rather similar sense of making sure people are listening, rather than distracting them with colour. I wonder if there's a sense around this time of concentrating on one dominant channel of meaning or sensation at a time. Of course, as sound itself becomes codified, the primary thing in the classical era becomes the story with dialogue - maybe this becomes so dominant that colour becomes marginalized and associated with the spectacular. There's then a long process by which colour - and we can see this in the history of Technicolor - becomes naturalized again as simply part of the storytelling rather than a spectacular element. There's a great deal of discussion about this in the thirties and forties.

Frank Kessler: Maybe we should in fact talk about the way colour is linked to the diegetic world, because stencil colouring is diegetic in the sense that the colours correspond to the colours of objects in that diegetic world, whereas tinting and toning are often non-diegetic. In explosions and night scenes the colour may well be diegetic, but need not be. The NAT PINKERTON example that has already been cited in this context is a very good case in point, because any reading of the colour as linked to the diegetic world eventually breaks down. The colour is sort of distanced from the diegetical world. Interestingly, in the example Sabine Lenk gave, Gorki reads the black-and-white as part of the diegetic world: that's a reading of black-and-white that disappears later on.

Heide Schlüpmann: Enno Patalas suggested that black-and-white reflected the photographic nature of cinema, but for me it's more to do with disregarding the audience and the place of cinema in the public sphere: withdrawing to the scientific and technical side of film, withdrawing into the private sphere. People were used to photography as black-and-white in the private sphere, but exhibited images, including the illustrated papers, tended toward colour. Exhibition is intimately bound up with colour, and if you talk about photography as black-and-white, you're talking about the private experience of photography. And this withdrawal into the scientific and technical aspects, and into the private sphere, leads to films made by auteurs.

Enno Patalas: What Heide says isn't entirely true, because the development of narration also makes colour less important. And narration is hardly 'anti-audience'. I think Griffith's Biographs were already released in black-and-white. They even said in the advertisements, in the publicity, that colour wasn't needed any more, because the photography was so advanced; but it was precisely these films that developed narration. The fact that tinting disappeared in the thirties has less to do with the technical aspects of the material than with the development of narration, which relegated spectacular effects to a subordinate role.

Tom Gunning: There's actually a fair amount of tinting in the Griffith films. We don't know whether the whole production was tinted or just some prints, but there are tinting indications in a lot of the Griffith Biographs. Mainly blue for night scenes, and metaphorical uses. In the print I've seen of THE BROKEN CROSS[9], for instance, I found tinting indications at every time the cross is shown. That shot had to be tinted gold to stress its emotional force.

9. THE BROKEN CROSS United States (Biograph) 1911

Nicholas Hiley: I arrived here, like Tom Gunning, with some very naive questions about colour, assuming among other things that it was a code you could somehow crack - that somehow blue-for-night and yellow-brown-for-lamplight and red-for-fire were just the first part of the code to have been cracked, and that beyond that it was all equally logical. We have, at the British Universities Film and Video Council in London, the issue-sheets for newsreels. The issue-sheets for British newsreels in the twenties list every story in each bi-weekly issue, and they note the tinting for each of these stories. I thought this would be very simple to crack, that you'd have one colour for sport, say, one for industry, one for politics and so on. But I couldn't find anything like that, although I did find a fire that was tinted red. The other thing that surprised me was that consecutive stories that were entirely different in character would have the same tint. The first four stories might be tinted lilac, even if these included a sporting story, say, or a political story. I came away wondering just what sort of order there was, and thinking maybe I was overlooking something like the fact that they'd made up a lot of lilac coloured dye, and decided to use it up. At least I'll leave here with some rather more sophisticated questions.

Why, for example, did colour disappear in the thirties and forties? I find this question very interesting because we have a hundred years of cinema, and most of

KIJKJES IN DENEMARKEN (Session 4) *nitrate*

DE LIEFDE VAN DEN BANDIET (Session 5) *nitrate*

DE LIEFDE VAN DEN BANDIET (Session 5) *nitrate*

DE LIEFDE VAN DEN BANDIET (Session 5) *nitrate*

it was coloured. So why was there this gap in the middle? That question leads to another: why did black-and-white disappear in the fifties and sixties? Some research has been done on this, suggesting that it was because of the competition from television, or from a domestic world which included television. The film-makers realized they were competing with this new medium, but could also sell it their old films; so if they made their new films in colour, they'd be able to sell them to the television companies after a few years of theatrical exhibition. This idea of competition may be related to what Heide Schlüpmann was saying about the context in which film appeared in the 1890s and 1900s. It had to compete with media that were coloured. Not only was screen practice highly coloured, but there was a world of colourful entertainment in which the new medium had to fight for market share. It's quite interesting that at the height of cinema attendance after the Second World War, when the cinema was more popular, at least in America, than it ever had been before or ever would be afterwards, when there was no great competition, the films were black-and-white. Perhaps we're concentrating too much on the aesthetics of colour, on the representational aspects of colour, and missing the economics: here's an added value you give to film, when you're competing with something else. When you're not competing with anything you can cut your costs by taking out the colour. Maybe we should talk a little more about the economics - not less about the aesthetics, but developing these two sets of questions side by side.

SESSION 4:
What's the Difference

Film programme:

PATHÉ'S ANIMATED GAZETTE 301B / *idem* / *idem* ❖ Great-Britain (Pathé) 1914 D2623 - 116m / video 073 - 6' ❖ black-and-white

PATHÉ COURANT 178A / PATHÉ NEWSREEL 178A / PATHÉ COURANT 178A ❖ The Netherlands (Pathé) [1912] ❖ DK1969 - 52m / video 362 - 3' ❖ tinting, black-and-white, toning, toning + tinting

BITS & PIECES NO.11 / *idem* / - ❖ United States ❖ DK1326 - 100m / video 009 - 5' tinting

DE KRUISSPIN / THE GARDEN SPIDER / [MOEURS DES ARAIGNÉES DES CHAMPS] France (Eclair) 1913 ❖ DK280 - 162m [original print length 178] / video 028 - 8' black-and-white, tinting

EENIGE EIGENAARDIGHEDEN IN HET LEVEN DER INSECTEN / SOME PECULIARITIES IN THE LIFE OF INSECTS / - ❖ [The Netherlands 1920] ❖ DK1972 - 65m / video 372 - 3' stencil

INDIA / *idem* / - ❖ France (Pathé) [1913] ❖ DK1602 - 48m / video 206 - 3' stencil

PARIJS, 11 NOVEMBER 1918 / PARIS, 11 NOVEMBER 1918 / - ❖ France (Pathé) 1918 ❖ D4846 - 52m / video 139 - 3' ❖ black-and-white

AFRIKA / AFRICA / - ❖ France [1922/1926] ❖ DK921 - 194m / video 354 - 10' stencilling

LICHAMELIJKE OEFENINGEN BESCHOUWD DOOR HET LANGZAAMWERKEND APPARAAT P.F. / PHYSICAL EXERCISES OBSERVED THROUGH THE SLOW MOTION CAMERA P.F. / ÉDUCATION PHYSIQUE ÉTUDIÉE AU RALENTISSEUR ❖ France (Pathé) 1915 ❖ DK314 - 137m / video 061 - 7' ❖ stencil

IN HET HOL VAN DE TOVERHEKS / IN THE WITCHES CAVE/ L'ANTRE DE LA SORCIERE France (Pathé) 1906 ❖ DK1348 - 107m (original print length 115m) / video 155 - 6' stencil

DE KIP MET DE GOUDEN EIEREN / THE HEN THAT LAYS THE GOLDEN EGGS/ LA POULE AUX OEUFS D'OR ❖ France (Pathé) 1905 Dir. Gaston Velle, Gabriel Moreau DK277 - 279m / video 315 - 14' ❖ toning, black-and-white, stencil, toning + stencil

KLEUR- EN VORMAFWISSELING OP 'CHOO-CHOO' JAZZ / COLOUR AND SHAPE VARIA-
TIONS ON 'CHOO-CHOO' JAZZ / KLEUR- EN VORMAFWISSELING OP 'CHOO-CHOO'
JAZZ ❖ The Netherlands 1932 Dir. Willem Bon ❖ DK1345 - 78m / video 155 - 4'
hand painting

CIRKELS / CIRCLES / KREISE ❖ Germany 1933 dir. Oskar Fischinger ❖ DK536 - 44m

SCHWECHATER / *idem* / *idem* ❖ Austria 1958 Dir. Peter Kubelka ❖ D177 - 30m

IN DE PYRENEEEN / IN THE PYRENEES / DANS LES PYRENÉES ❖ France (Gaumont)
1913 ❖ DK526 - 52m (original print length 57m) / video 027 - 3' ❖ tinting + stencil

LOETSCHBERG / *idem* / LE CHEMIN DE FER DE LOETSCHBERG ❖ France (Eclipse)
1913 ❖ DK312 - 83m (original print length 157m) / video 062 - 4' ❖ tinting

KIJKJES IN DENEMARKEN / GLIMPSES OF DENMARK / - ❖ [Norway, 1915] ❖ DK322 -
82m / video 144 - 5' ❖ toning, tinting

IN JAPAN / *idem* / - ❖ Japan (The Japanese Film) [1913] ❖ DK972 - 141m / video
031 - 7' ❖ black-and-white

IN EGYPTE / IN EGYPT / - ❖ France (Pathé) [1920] ❖ DK385 - 184m ❖ tinting,
toning, toning + tinting

ZWEDEN MET ZIJN PRACHTIG NATUURSCHOON / SWEDEN AND ITS SUPERB NATURAL
BEAUTY / - ❖ [Sweden/The Netherlands 1919] ❖ DK1970 - 103m / video 362 - 5'
tinting, toning, stencil

SANTA-LUCIA / *idem* / - ❖ [Italy (Ambrosio) 1910] ❖ DK282 - 97m / video 124 - 6'
tinting, toning, black-and-white

M oderator **Jacques Aumont**: I know of no subject more difficult to discuss
than colour, so we must choose our words very carefully, and remain constantly aware of the complexity of the task we've set ourselves. Let me begin by
returning briefly to some questions already raised in earlier sessions. People have
been asking what we should do with all this coloured material in the archives. I
won't here address questions of preservation, because I'm personally more interested in questions of exhibition. Why should this material be shown not only to
specialized audiences such as this one, but to more general audiences? What is the
point? So far, I've heard three kinds of answers to this question. The first sort of
answer is that we should show it because it adds to our knowledge of the past. I
don't want to call this a 'historical' approach, because all our discussions here are
historically determined by both subject-matter and our own perspective. So
leaving aside, at least provisionally, the dichotomy between 'historical' and

'ahistorical' approaches to colour, one minimal answer is that we show these films in the hope that they'll help people understand something of their own past. Perhaps I can illustrate what I mean by taking a distant parallel. Medievalists tell us that at some point in the twelfth century there was a sort of revolution in chromatic taste, at least in western countries, with blue replacing red as the dominant colour, the colour of kings. This is demonstrated by the textual analysis of written documents. But wouldn't we see this better if we had films from the twelfth century? To put things very naively, we can't deprive people of this means of access to changes in mentalities at the beginning of our century. And this sort of answer seems to imply that archives or museums should show films as they were made. But we're all, of course, aware of the danger of talking about 'films as they were originally': nobody knows exactly what this means.

The second sort of answer has to do with taste, 'We show it because we like it' - and this is basically the approach taken by the Nederlands Filmmuseum here in Amsterdam. It's a very significant approach, whose importance must be emphasized. Taste is very important historically, socially, ideologically. We are all aware of this, and questions of taste are to me just as important as questions of knowledge. The two sets of questions sometimes converge, but sometimes they diverge. An archive like the Filmmuseum treats this early material as found footage - 'We find something interesting, so we show it to people, and sometimes we organize what we find to suggest aesthetic ideas'. I could say a lot about the historicity of this taste. Many people in earlier sessions evoked the taste for black-and-white in older archives. I personally was raised in the archive of Henri Langlois, who believed only in black-and-white, in films without music, and very often in films without intertitles. Sometimes he even cut the flash-titles from the prints he showed to a very frustrated general audience. He had a taste for photographic reality, for a touch of surrealism, for a very content-oriented approach toward this material and, of course, for an auteurist approach.

There's a third answer, which I prefer to these first two: that this material is interesting in the precise measure that it helps us form ideas about colour in general and images in general, and about the cinematic image in particular. These early films are interesting as containing what I will call 'colour-events'. It's not a very precise term, but it should at least help pinpoint what I'm trying to get at. To talk about events allows me to avoid talking about things like intentions or coherence, systems or meanings. What interests me in these films is nothing to do with any possible 'colour system'. The colours probably don't mean very much, but they may tell us a lot about ideas of colour. One of the most striking examples of what I'm trying to get at is the shot in SANTA LUCIA where the film has been decaying or solarizing. What is perhaps most striking is the way this enhances the shot where there's a sort of yellow ghost floating over a familiar panorama of Venice. One of the advantages of early film in this respect is that colour-events are more crude, more brutal than in later films and sometimes more intense. I don't exactly know the reason for this, but it may be related to the fact that there's less colour in early films then in later ones. Someone suggested there was some sort of equivalence between colouring and the close-up, but perhaps there's actually a broader equivalence between colour and dramatic elements in general.

What kind of colour events have we seen so far? A very great variety. But rather than attempting any sort of list or catalogue, let me take a few examples. An 'event', of course, suggests the idea of time, and perhaps the most obvious kind of colour-event in early films is the sudden appearance of colour. My first example is the unexpected appearance of floating patches of colour on some dresses in THE GREAT TRAIN ROBBERY[1]. The appearance was for me unexpected in various senses, since I know this film very well, but only in black-and-white. Seeing it with added colour was in itself a small shock. So the sudden appearance of colour at that point in the print we saw here was for me also the sudden appearance of colour in a more general sense.

1. Session 1

The sudden appearance of colour very often takes a far more stereotypical and coded form in the 'final highlight' of many of the films shown here - the penulti-mate shot of THE MOST BEAUTIFUL FANS OF THE WORLD[2], for instance, with its golden waterfall, really impressed and engaged me - but this sort of irruption of colour is perhaps weaker as an event. Colour helps to 'sculpt time', to draw on a metaphor coined in the twenties, or helps to turn time into music, to take an even more common twenties metaphor. Perhaps it even contributes to what some Germans around 1925 were calling 'absolute film'.

2. Session 1: DE MOOISTE WAAIERS TER WERELD / THE MOST BEAUTIFUL FANS IN THE WORLD

A second way that colour helps create events is by articulating objects and space. This is perhaps less obvious. Frank Kessler asked in Session 3 whether we really perceive a world of objects rather than some cultural construct. This is a very broad question, an anthropological question, and as far as I'm aware, there's precious little literature by anthropologists or ethnologists on perception - which is a pity, because it's now almost too late to undertake such cross-cultural research. From the few studies I've seen, it's difficult to draw any conclusions, but it's clear that cultures differ in the way they apply mental categories to objects in the world.

Now, film presents us with something like another layer or an iteration of this perceptual filter, though we must make a fundamental distinction, in the context of these early films, between the two major ways of colouring films. Monochromatic colouring tends to dissolve the distinction between object and space, figure and ground. Thus in HARAKIRI[3], the human figure is sometimes lost against the background of the shot - lost among the rocks, in the sand, in the visual form or texture of the film. In some shots human figures become just a granulation of the film. Hand-painting or stencilling, on the other hand, tends to produce patches of colour floating in front of objects and blurring their shape. This 'free-floating' colour becomes more or less independent of the objects 'behind' it, which is rather eery. If we think about this phenomenologically, abstracting from everything we know about the production of the image and so

3. Evening Programme, Wednesday 26 July: HARAKIRI

on, we might wonder how we can even identify the colourless objects behind these floating colours. We can make sense of such a world, but it remains very strange. Sometimes in this strange world, colours do become more tightly attached to objects. In the fashion films of the Opening Programme there were umbrellas, or elaborately embroidered lady's bags, that suddenly took on their own relief and colour because they had such a strong shape, such affirmative existence in space. On a perceptual level, colour generally seems to possess an independent material existence, more or less detached from the objects represented in these films. I've always seen this, and ever more strongly see it, as the strange lesson to be learnt from these films: the autonomy of colour, the independence of colours and things.

Then there are experiences or events in these films associated with *light*, simply as light. Colour dims the light or events with light. It's one of the big arguments in favour of black-and-white film. I want to avoid value-judgements, but it's true that added colour in film is not 'natural' colour, not tied to light as it is in the 'natural' world around us. We attach colours to objects within our specific cultural grid, but they're 'naturally' attached - so to speak - to light. Our sensation of colour derives from the way our ocular and nervous system processes light, but in early films colour and light became detached from each other, particularly in hand-painted films. Here again, there are important aesthetic differences between toning and hand-colouring: with toning a certain natural quality of light is preserved. This struck me very forcibly watching the shots of the snow in GLIMPSES OF DENMARK, where all of a sudden you get a vast amount of white in the image. I initially perceived this as light, as the reflection of sunlight, or maybe moonlight, on ice. But then, as the shot became whiter and still whiter, the whiteness eventually turned for me from being light into being pure white. And it's very unusual to experience this degree of subjective response to an image in films of a later period. Indeed - to summarize my remarks so far - the fundamental difference between these films and the other films that inhabit our memory is that in these early films the colours or colour-events tend to be more or less independent of the represented scene. And I should perhaps emphasize that this colour is not just colour in general, but a specifically cinematic colour. One thing that strikes me again and again when I see monochrome is that the monochrome we see in films produced between, say, 1906 or 1908 and 1930, isn't exactly the use of colour - and for me this comes out much more strongly in film than in still images. I've always felt that monochromes in film, monochrome shots, are more a way of avoiding the question of colour than solving it. A shot in one colour is not exactly a coloured shot. The colour may be used to give some particular meaning to the shot, and this is then the only meaning of the colour. This is particularly obvious with red, but we might equally well discuss the use of, say, lilac. And then you get single colours that seem to last forever, in Griffith films like BROKEN BLOSSOMS[4],

for example, which has very little colour variation, with only three colours in all - it's really a monochrome. You lose the sense that it's in colour.

4. BROKEN BLOSSOMS United
States 1919

On the most general level, I would simply say that these films use colour to establish differences in the image, and for me the differences that colour introduces or reproduces in an image are as fundamental as any other element. And I'm very tempted to see in some of these films a deliberate experimentation with colour, grain, sharpness, texture, and so on. Furthermore, and in conclusion, I think we should see the experiments or discoveries in this dimension of film - which I would call 'colour-ideas' - echoed, despite their obvious historicity, travel over the whole history of film. To range very widely over that history, we might take as a striking example Ingmar Bergman's PASSION[5] . This, for me, is one of Bergman's most fascinating films, because it's a vast experiment with colour, texture, grain, focus, and so on - a vast experiment with the figuration of the cinematic image. And I see the same sort of thing in these early films - 'colour-ideas' that anybody, whether filmmakers or film scholars, can take up and elaborate in their own way. Of course - to conclude my conclusion - people have been doing this for a long time, and to leave the scholars aside for the moment, I'll end with a personal tribute to the many film artists in the past and the present who have worked or are working with the colour of early film, trying to think it, and think with it. As Mariann Lewinsky put it so well, colour is now.

5. EN PASSION / PASSION Sweden 1969

Jürgen Reble: I particularly agree with what you say about the autonomous existence of colour in film. For me this is a physical existence with a life of its own. In the films we've seen colour is linked to the physical structure of the objects filmed. I myself work a lot with these old techniques of toning and tinting, but I try to use these systems to create new forms and new colours in the film material. If I have an image which already has a physical structure determined by the shooting, in the camera, then I try to reorganize this material so that the colour takes on a life or structure of its own. It's an autonomous element of the image and, in a way, has nothing to do with the colour on the surface of the things that were filmed. In fact, when we use colour film stock to film some real surface, there's actually more illusion than with black-and-white stock, because a black-and-white image is much closer to the physical structure of what we see. So the idea that colour is only a quality of the film material is very interesting. The most interesting thing in these films was to see how colour takes on its own life, independently of the things that are filmed, or that we see around us. I see it as a special, new layer of the film, completely separate from the other elements. As a filmmaker using these sorts of process, working directly on the film material, working with the colour on an artistic level, rather than as an illusionistic or representational device, I don't add colours to make the image more attractive or more visually pleasurable, but to express an emotional relation to the image.

Péter Forgács: Colour sometimes conveys a special message, nothing didactic, but something that was hiding in the moving image. One thing I learnt at last year's Workshop was that there was really no such thing as a 'black-and-white' period of film, or that black-and-white and other versions of monochrome were just one kind of colouring. And listening now to Jacques Aumont, I can imagine Wittgenstein sitting here enjoying these coloured black-and-white pictures, because he was always asking whether, say, this red was really red. We could see these jumping stencilled colours as a kind of superimposed animation. I'm amused by 'mistakes' in film: by scratches, by 'incorrect' colouring, by this 'other layer' on the film, this other film. Colour has its own life. Maybe it was added to sell the films, or to convey a special message, but what I see is a special layer of film, or two films, three films, at the same time.

But I have a bit of a problem with the discussion here. I wonder whether it's not a - brave - mistake to try to speak about the colour of the films and not speak about the music, because the colour and the music and the written text are just three dimensions of the 'film text' as a whole. We can't know how people at the time saw these films, we can only see them from our own contemporary perspectives of auteur, scholar, or archivist. If 'colour is now' in this sense, then shouldn't we be discussing colour in terms of the more general question of how a film is constituted from these three elements? To put it very simply, if you add music to a flower, the meaning changes. It can change so much that it distorts my perception - and it's the same with colour.

Don McWilliams: This question of music is interesting. Ideally, you'd be able to create music and film together. The music for BEGONE DULL CARE[6] was written beforehand, with a very specific idea of the film in mind, and then McLaren literally painted to the music. He always thought in terms of simultaneity, but you can probably only work that way in abstract film. Oskar Fischinger tried it too. It would be wonderful if somehow with live action, we could get the music first, then get footage matching the emotions in the music, and colour matching too. One feels limited, constrained, by the current technology; perhaps with electronic colorization we'll be able to do much more manipulation. I've tried a lot in the lab, but you feel imprisoned. The only real experiment I've done in this area was when McLaren and I found one of his lost films in black-and-white. Using mattes and applied colour and filters we actually created a colour film. It's interesting that with the current 'old' technology, one basically has to go back to black-and-white and start again; perhaps with new technology we'll be able to really work in colour.

6. Session 2: BEGONE DULL CARE

Albert Wulffers: For me, looking at these films, and at the primary colours in more recent films like Godard's MADE IN U.S.A.[7], or Derek Jarman's BLUE[8], there's not so much meaning in these colours. It doesn't really add anything to what I see. If I make a distinction between tinting and toning on the one hand, and hand painting and stencilling on the other, then having been trained as a graphic designer, I don't find tinting and toning very interesting, they don't really add much to the image. Tinting, to me, is like what you do in graphic design when you've only got enough money for

7. MADE IN U.S.A. France/Italy 1967

8. BLUE Great-Britain 1993

black-and-white printing, so to make it a little more fancy you use red paper. For me these films are like a soccer-club or church magazine. In high-school they made our 'blackboards' green, because it was supposed to be better for our eyes, but this didn't change the information on the board, for me it was still a blackboard; changing the colour only changes the mood.

Toning is a bit different. When I see a black-and white film toned in some colour I have a feeling of incompleteness, because as soon as I see a black-and-white image in blue, I miss all the other colours. In a way, I have all those colours in my head. With one colour it's like one of the four different plates you make when you're printing a poster - that's the feeling I get when I see toning.

I like hand-colouring and stencilling much better. Here again, there's a further distinction between the more realistic stencilling you see in travelogues, where they try to make the image more like what we see with our own eyes, and the more artificial approach you get in more theatrical images, which I like best of all. It's a technique I could myself imagine using in a film, because by putting a colour in one particular place you can introduce more framing within the overall frame that's already there. You get this in painting, in a Warhol portrait or a Léger canvas. Léger dissociates the colour from the contours in a drawing, so it's linked to the black-and-white image but still an independent element. That's the sort of thing you can do with stencils.

Tom Gunning: Jacques Aumont returns us so vividly to the act of seeing. I bring that up because the inclusion of SCHWECHATER in the film programme represents a filmmaker who really taught me to see in a new way. Peter Kubelka makes a direct contrast between himself as a filmmaker and a medieval or renaissance painter. A renaissance painter, he would say, got a beautiful blue by grinding up lapis lazuli, and combining it with sensual material like brandy and eggs. He, on the other hand, exposes film in a camera then gets it back from Kodak with a blue that makes him throw up. He hasn't got the same intense relationship to colour as a painter.

There are two points that I'd like to make about this. Kubelka felt he couldn't use colour as powerfully as other artists in other media, but that film was a really powerful medium for exploring time. One's struck in SCHWECHATER not so much by the beauty of what used - at least - to be red, but by the relation of the colour to time, and the way there's some particular sound, a hum or beep, whenever the red appears seems to me a perfect example of the 'now-ness' of colour. And this raises again the important fact that we're isolating colour in order to talk about it, we're trying to talk about it, but it's interrelated with all sorts of other structures, with temporality in particular.

My second point about Kubelka's remark echoes something Giovanna Fossati said in Session 1 - that with present-day colour stock you can't get some colours together. If you save the pink, that distorts the other colours. The colour stock already embodies a certain ideology of colour, of certain balances and limits. One very striking thing about early nitrate films is that they in some sense violate certain ideas of colour balance and harmony and can do this because they're 'hand-made'. All this is important, though I wouldn't want to push it towards some idea of an artistic cinema in the control of auteurs, because another very striking thing is how casual a lot of the colouring decisions seem to be. In contrast to Kubelka's films, which are wonderfully calculated, these early films derive some of their power from this rather offhand approach, this playful freedom.

Jacques Aumont: Most of what I like in these films is accidental. The absolute white in GLIMPSES OF DENMARK wasn't meant to be there; the yellow ghost of decay or solarisation in SANTA LUCIA is accidental; the sudden change of colour in the dress in THE GREAT TRAIN ROBBERY is accidental. We have very perverse tastes because we can't of course watch these films 'innocently' - that's totally out of the question. So we have to find a way to relate to them in some way, and my personal approach is an aesthetic one.

Tom Gunning: Yes, while intentions are certainly present in some of these films, particularly the later ones, they're very often secondary. It's curious that when I talk to other film scholars about colour in silent film they immediately want to know who made various decisions. Of course, I too want to know whether the auteur or somebody else decided something - but it was nearly always someone else. The interesting thing about the question is that it shows how the colour or colourfulness of these early films seems to convey certain types of intention. These can of course become other people's intentions as they pick them up - and this aspect of found objects is really quite important.

Mariann Lewinsky: On tinting and the question of what it adds and how it creates events in a film, I'd say that tinting greatly softens the ghostly directness of black-and-white, the skeletal aspect of black-and-white, and gives the image air and space. It makes the experience of seeing slightly more emotional - not in a purposeful or simply narrative way, but rather as saying, 'Here is something nice to see', which is a response with no specific connotation. This works best with light green or yellow, or light brown or orange, but is more difficult with cold browns and blues, because there isn't enough warmth, and they're too specific in their effect. Within those constraints you can in fact be very arbitrary as an archivist colouring a film. If our culture generally attaches colour too closely to objects, then it partly redeems this culture that it's produced these films, because in them we see a completely different use of colour.

Nicola Mazzanti: One striking thing, particularly in feature films, is how you somehow become blind to the colour. After twenty minutes of yellow in FOOLISH WIVES[9] you become 'yellow-blind'. Maybe we should talk about this additive colour-blindness in monochrome films. When you see a restored print on the screen, you may find yourself gasping 'Oh my god, the intertitles are in different colours'. But then you measure them with a densitometer and find the intertitles coloured the same all the way through. A yel-

9. FOOLISH WIVES United States (Universal) 1922 Dir. Erich von Stroheim

low scene or blue scene makes you yellow-blind or blue-blind, so when you suddenly see the orange, it looks different.

Maybe we should also talk about the 'freedom' of early colour, about freedom and experimentation. We may see this freedom as offhand, casual, something that allows you to put a single sepia-toned shot within a long yellow-tinted sequence, without implying any particular meaning. But this may be wrong. THE HEN THAT LAYS THE GOLDEN EGGS is the third print of this film that I've seen, all from different nitrates, with the stencilled colours at exactly the same places, apart from a few very minor differences. The colouring of this kind of film was very precisely organized. Each piece of negative was separated, marked with a number or the name of a colour or a code, then colour-processed in another department, coming back with the right colour to be edited, combined with all the other pieces in the right order to get a final positive print. It was very difficult to interfere in this process, because nothing in the process was actually casual, except some occasional mistake or the dyes becoming too dilute so you got a pale instead of a strong colour. We have to be careful talking about 'freedom' in such a strictly organized industrial process.

One other thing is that if we move on to classic films, the truth is that we just don't know very much about the colour. We know pretty well how Ambrosio coloured documentary shots in 1911, but if we think about NOSFERATU[10] and other German classics, or most Italian classics, even FOOLISH WIVES, a lot of work has been done on the texts, but nothing much on the colour. And we have very little information to work on. Most nitrate has been lost - maybe we still have second release prints, or a black-and-white print, but that's it. We only have information about one level of colouring, the automatic colouring of most of these productions that obviously reflects some specific taste. And a taste that's not always easy to understand: why, precisely, is the towel to the left of the man drinking coffee coloured yellow? Why the towel rather than something else, when the rest is left black-and-white? Why change black-and-white to sepia, or from tinting to toning, or vice-versa? We rarely know why and where these decisions were made. We can of course still think about not so much a code, but an aesthetic or a taste that changes radically over a short period. I see a lot of differences between a stencilled film of 1905 and a stencilled film of 1911. It's a different world. With feature films, along with the short films we're seeing here, things changed very fast.

10. NOSFERATU Germany (Prana-Film) 1921 Dir. Friedrich Wilhelm Murnau

Peter Delpeut: I'm not so sure about this 'colour blindness' effect. You may stop being conscious of the colour, but it always has some physical effect. Editing THE FORBIDDEN QUEST[11], we had black-and-white scenes that we had shot and monochrome archival footage. On the working print, we got a very annoying effect. Cutting from the archival monochrome to the black-and-white shots, we'd get the monochrome colour sort of persisting in the black-and-white. That made me realize that monochrome colour has a

11. THE FORBIDDEN QUEST The Netherlands 1994 Dir. Peter Delpeut

very strong physical effect. Maybe you forget it, but it's still there, something is happening between your body and the screen. There's more to colour than something we can interpret as we watch a film, there's something physical too.

Eric de Kuyper: I'd like to return to the problem of colour and light. There's a real problem with monochrome in the way you lose light. But it seems that 'they', whoever that may have been, were very conscious of this and played with the contrast in less light or fuzzy light. A shot in a monochrome film with a silhouette in the foreground, or framed by a dark mask, makes the rest of the shot seem lighter - which is an illusion of course. In WAR BE DAMNED[12] for instance, you get full-frame red monochrome shots, then you get a dark 'binocular' mask, which suddenly makes the image much more brilliant. Franz Hofer based the mise en scene of his HEIDENRÖSCHEN[13] on this sort of frame-within-a-frame.

12. Session 1: VERVLOEKT ZIJ DEN OORLOG / WAR BE DAMNED

13. KLEIN HEIDEROOSJE / HEIDENRÖSCHEN Germany (Luna Film) 1916

In a lot of monochrome films from the twenties you do sometimes lose any sense of the colour. But in the early teens there was this kind of yellow, for example: working with coloured nitrate for five years, I'd almost fall asleep during the greens, but when this yellow appeared, I'd suddenly wake up again, feeling that something was happening. This is true to a lesser degree with red, and even with blue you don't become colour-blind but more perverse, as if collecting Delftware. Someone who doesn't know about Delft sees only 'blue', but there are thousands of blues. You become very sensitive to these colours, but that of course is a present-day perversion. Anyway, there are dull colours, and there are very happy colours that do something with the image.

What I miss in what we've seen here are stencilled feature films: the programme gives the impression that stencilling was mainly used in travelogues and *féerique* films. I especially miss Léonce Perret and other authors of the early teens like Alfred Machin - in Perret's comedies of Machin's dramas there's a very interesting use of stencil colour. We haven't really talked quite enough about stencilling.

Jacques Aumont: In response to Nicola Mazzanti and Eric de Kuyper - something else that has been missing so far in this discussion of colour is the name of Goethe. We're heavily indebted to Goethe's theory of colours, whether we know it or not, and what Eric de Kuyper just said was thoroughly Goethian: there are happy colours, melancholy colours, dull colours; this could have come straight from the pages of Goethe's magisterial work. And we might expand on Péter Forgács' reference to Wittgenstein, though his approach was quite different. Wittgenstein was primarily addressing questions of language rather than colour. I have of course read his essay on colour, and I've derived very few ideas about colour from him - and many ideas about language. Goethe is the prime reference. This isn't just a historical or cultural aside: Goethe's thesis that colour isn't an aspect of light but of shadow might explain the response to the monochrome of early films. It's no conclusion, it's a statement.

A few more remarks about monochrome. Monochrome is a good area in which to explore the transfer of chromatic ideas from early to contemporary film. The monochrome red in Nicholas Ray's BIGGER THAN LIFE of 1956 echoes the classical use of red as a signal for danger, for emotion, for internal burning. It's very similar to the beautiful red shots of firemen fighting a blaze in the last session. But then the monochromes at the beginning of Godard's CONTEMPT[14] have a totally different visual texture. They produce a totally different effect - they are more transparent. There's the celebrated shot of Bardot's naked body on the bed, using filters. The red filter at the beginning of CONTEMPT produces a lighter red than you get in Ray's film, and you have the sense that the scene is taking place behind something: it's not so much tinted as filtered. Some recent films have used monochrome lighting - a very celebrated example is Fassbinder's LOLA[15], where the blue monochromes produce yet another effect, because the relief is not lost with this technique.

14. LE MÉPRIS / CONTEMPT France 1963

15. LOLA Germany 1978

So monochrome has gone through many variations in the history of film, and I'd be at a loss to draw one conclusion from all these monochromatic experiences. But I do have the feeling that monochrome is somehow always the negation of colour, always amounts to an attempt to negate the specific power of colour. Either by pushing colour toward some meaning, as in Ray's film, or toward the absence of meaning, as in the Fassbinder film. Each tries to draw us into a world where chromatic experience is denied. I wouldn't expect Eric de Kuyper to agree with me here; we seem to have a very different sensibility to colour.

Anarchy, but not without Order

Film programme:

DE LIEFDE VAN DEN BANDIET / THE BANDIT'S LOVE / THE GREATER LOVE ❖ United States of America (Vitagraph) 1912 Dir. Rollin S. Sturgeon ❖ DK47 - 294m / video 338 - 15' ❖ tinting

exerpt from: OVERWINNEN OF STERVEN / VICTORY OR DEATH / VITTORIA O MORTE Italy (Itala) 1913 ❖ DK852 - 829m (original print length 1400m) / video 046 - 38' tinting

HET VANGEN VAN ZEEHONDEN OP DE BANKEN VAN NEW-FOUNDLAND / SEAL HUNTING ON THE NEWFOUNDLAND BANKS / - ❖ Canada [1915] ❖ DK1971 - 238m / video 257 - 12' ❖ toning + tinting, tinting, black-and-white

exerpt from: BIJ DE LAPPEN IN NOORD-ZWEDEN / AMONG THE LAPPS IN NORTH SWEDEN / - ❖ [France] (Pathé) [1923] ❖ DK882 - 483m / video 142 - 24' ❖ tinting, toning

LAPLAND IN DE WINTER / LAPLAND IN WINTER / - ❖ [Sweden 1915] ❖ DK321 - 75m / video 098 - 4' ❖ toning

exerpt from: IN HET NOORDPOOLGEBIED / IN THE ARCTIC / CAPTAIN F.E. KLEIN-SCHMIDT'S ARCTIC HUNT ❖ United States of America 1914 Dir. Frank E. Kleinschmidt ❖ DK838 - 629m / video 028 - 31' ❖ tinting, toning

PANORAMA VAN RUSLAND: DE CASPISCHE ZEE / PANORAMA OF RUSSIA: THE CASPIAN ZEE / SUR LA MER CASPIENNE ❖ France (Gaumont) [1912] ❖ DK685 - 52m / video 027 - 3' ❖ tinting, toning, toning + tinting

BITS & PIECES NO.195 / *idem* / - ❖ DK1398 - 40m/ video 299 - 2' ❖ [pre-tinting, toning]

DE VLIEGMACHINE DER GEBROEDERS MOREAU MET AUTOMATISCHE EVENWICHTS-HOUDER / THE MOREAU BROTHERS' AIRPLANE WITH AUTOMATIC BALANCER / L'AÉROSTABLE DES FRERES MOREAU ❖ France (Gaumont) [1913] ❖ D3678 - 72m (original print length 76m) / video 075 - 4' ❖ black-and-white

BITS & PIECES NO.35 / *idem* / THE GOOD PROVIDER ❖ United States of America 1922 Dir. Frank Borzage ❖ DK558 - 160m / video 009 - 8' ❖ tinting

RAPOLLO / RAPALLO / *idem* ❖ Italy (Cines) 1914 ❖ DK957 - 75m / video 124 - 4' stencil, tinting + stencil

LIMBURG IN BEELD: MAASTRICHT / PICTURES OF LIMBURG: MAASTRICHT /
LIMBURG IN BEELD: MAASTRICHT ❖ The Netherlands (Hollandia Film) 1918-1919
Dir. Jules Stoop ❖ DK1451 - 357m / video 251 - 18' ❖ tinting, toning, toning +
tinting

DE GEHEIMZINNIGE ZUSTERS / THE MYSTERIOUS SISTERS / DEN SCHWARZE KUGEL
ODER DIE GEHEIMNISVOLLEN SCHWESTERN ❖ Germany (Luna Film) 1913 Dir. Franz
Hofer ❖ exerpt from: D2751 - 456m ❖ black-and-white ❖ DK807 - 690m / video
053 - 31' ❖ tinting, toning

EEN TREURSPEL IN DE BIOSCOOP / A TRAGEDY IN THE CINEMA / UNA TRAGEDIA AL
CINEMATOGRAFO ❖ Italy (Cines) 1913 ❖ DK51 - 151m / video 053 - 8' ❖ tinting

Moderator **Peter Delpeut** : I want to concentrate in this session on a specific
fiction film to compensate for what may be their under-representation in
the overall programme of films shown at this Workshop. I've chosen THE GREATER
LOVE, which opened today's screening, more or less at random, and I'll use what
we call a 'research quality' video copy to pursue the analysis, but my argument
properly relates, of course, to the safety print from which the video was produced.
I won't attempt anything like a full analysis, but I hope we can learn something
about how monochrome colour works by looking in a little more detail at a particular monochrome film.

The first shot is orange - or should we call it yellow?[1]
It's always very difficult at the beginning of a film to see
what the colour might mean, because you have no idea
what's coming next. But my initial association here
would be with sunlight, an outdoor scene, a very soft
colour-reference to an exterior. And it's interesting in this first scene that there's
no change of colour between shots - this produces some kind of continuity.

1. A sequence of frame stills is
reproduced between pages 48
and 49

When we change to the villain's viewpoint a little later on, there's a spatial transition that might have motivated a change of colour; the fact there's no such
change suggests, on a narrative level, a connection between the two places.

Nico de Klerk: As well as the colour having a kind of a referential meaning -
outdoor sunlight - couldn't the fact that the shot from the villain's viewpoint is
the same colour could be motivated by the act of looking, a shared narrative
world? There may be two separate places, but each can be seen from the other.

Peter Delpeut: Later in the film, the first interior shot is in 'neutral' black-and-
white - although with so many colours, you might wonder whether black-and-
white is altogether neutral.

Tom Gunning: Yellow tinting is usually the indication for artificial interior
light. This is inverted here because it has already been used for an exterior scene,

which is strange. One association of this yellow, which is perhaps more yellow or golden - almost orange - than most 'interior' yellow tints for light, may be with the West, the intensity of 'western' outdoor light; people often talked in those days of 'the golden west'. Vitagraph didn't do many westerns and might have wanted to get this association at the outset.

As for the transition from gold to black-and-white, we have to consider the role of colour contrasts. Since a transition from gold to yellow would probably not be noticed, black-and-white might have been the only other option here. If gold had already been used to indicate genre and geographical location, then yellow wasn't really an option, and the next best thing would be black-and-white.

Mariann Lewinsky: Yellow can be used for either natural or artificial light, but we should also consider the overall economy of colouring. Here we have lots of exterior shots, more exteriors than interiors, and it would make sense to use the 'yellow-for-light' outside. If you used it for interiors, you'd need another colour for the exteriors and you'd lose the general golden flavour of the film.

Peter Delpeut: OK, these are various options that are in some sense external to the film. But the film's only just begun and there's no system yet. The film will in fact construct a system of its own. So let's get a bit further before we identify this yellow too much with the golden west.

Next we get a colour we all like, because it's 'non-referential': purple. It has a symbolic value, or rather a connotative value. You begin by associating it with the love scene, but then the love scene develops into a jealousy scene. So what does the colour really convey?

Frank Kessler: We're going a little too fast here, reading colours simply in terms of meaning or semantics. The colours actually function in quite a complex way. In the first place, we have to consider not only the system of colours them-selves, but the system of colour *changes* too, regardless which colour changes to which. You might see the yellow or orange opening sequence as simply the intro-duction of the various characters. Then the black-and-white shot shows the beginning of the conflict in jealousy. Then you get the evolution of this with the alternation of blue and orange in the night scene. There's some sort of narrative segmentation in the colour changes. There's a link to the diegetic world - on the simplest level to some temporal order: first daylight, then the interior scene, then later that day, then a night scene, a dawn scene, another midday. There's this temporal articulation, but it's fundamentally narrative articulation: the introduc-tion, the beginning of conflict, the sharpening of conflict, the alternation over-night, the showdown, and the ending, all marked by colour changes.

Peter Delpeut: But can't the colour have both a referential and a symbolic value at the same time?

TOLL OF THE SEA(Evening programme, 28 July) *acetate*

IN HET NOORDPOOLGEBIED (Session 5) *nitrate*

FEEENDANS (Session 1) *nitrate*

VALSE TRISTE (Session 2) *acetate*

Frank Kessler: Of course it has multiple meanings, plays on different levels. One should try to keep in mind the different layers of meaning and the articulative force of the colours.

Heide Schlüpmann: I'm not very happy with all this discussion of the way the colour refers to the external world, to sunlight or narrative elements. For me colour has more to do with internal things like sensations and the sensitivity of the viewer; not just with the optical sensitivity of the eyes, but an inner sensitivity. Maybe we should talk about colouring time rather than space. There's no problem with the yellow afternoon in the opening sequence, we can all remember an afternoon as yellow; but you could remember an afternoon as purple if there was some sort of dissonance in it. A yellow afternoon and a blue night may seem straightforward enough at first, but we might remember them as purple.

To talk about colouring time is to talk about colouring strips of film or colouring the time of the film, which isn't just some mechanical process, because from one frame to the next it's fundamentally *time* that we experience, and time, therefore, that we're colouring. I'd really like to stress that.

Nico de Klerk: To return to the purple scene, the length of the purple, gives the audience almost the time to try to give some kind of meaning to the changes in the scene.

Peter Delpeut: But the strange thing is that because the purple lasts so long, it becomes 'difficult'. When it first appears you really feel 'Ah', and it really adds something to the story. But the longer it lasts the more difficult it becomes to link it to any definite feeling or narrative development.

Eric de Kuyper: This kind of discussion and analysis makes me rather uneasy, although it's a very interesting sort of experiment. But we're forgetting something very important, which is the fact that we've been watching colour films for three days now, and personally, when I see this opening yellow scene of THE GREATER LOVE I remember all the other yellows I've seen over the last few days. It reminds me particularly of the yellow street in A TRAGEDY IN THE CINEMA. We can't really look as innocently as people seem to be implying at these images. Our minds are full of colourful images, just as the minds of the original audiences probably were. They were living among these kinds of colours. So what we're trying to do now is rather like a classroom exercise or a laboratory experiment, trying to forget the whole colourful context from which these images emerged, and from which they've been re-emerging these last days. We're already working with an unconscious system of colours, built up these last few days and before. Built up by us not only as scholars, but also as spectators.

Frieda Grafe: What I've experienced here these last few days is the change in colour which occurred with film. The colour we're seeing here isn't the colour we experience in paintings or in reality, but colour as transformed by the photographic image. We're too tied to the colour we know, when we write about colour; too accustomed to see colour in an art-historical context. Film really gave a new sort of impulse to colour. Cinematic colour is different, it's an experience.

Jacques Aumont: We each have our own experience of the colour in these films. As Eric de Kuyper says, we've been immersed in colour here, like much earlier audiences. What particularly strikes me about the lilac in the present film - actually purple on video, but lighter on the projection print - is how my experience of this colour, in the context of the other early tinted films we've seen here, is essentially intertextual. For me, this lilac resonates directly with the lilac in other fiction films. The first one that comes to my mind is the lilac of BROKEN BLOSSOMS[2] because it also comes quite 'out of the blue' so to speak. In each case lilac suddenly appears for no apparent reason, it's initially just incomprehensible. For me, this was very moving in the Griffith film, because it's a passionate scene. I very much agree with Heide Schlüpmann that such colouring has an intense emotional quality - and 'means' very little else. And this emotional quality carries over into other films. The lilac here is all the other lilacs I've seen too. What can we say about the power of these colours? They still suprise us, here, because for most of us this colour is a new experience. But how much did they surprise the original audiences? Or, since I vowed to avoid that question, let me turn it around: was this lilac, say, becoming a cliché by the time this film was made, a stereotype, or was it, then too, the sudden appearance of an unexpected colour?

2. BROKEN BLOSSOMS United States 1919 Dir. D.W. Griffith

Peter Delpeut: The key thing is to see that there was no fixed code. There was intertextuality of course, a memory of colours in other films, and maybe this is a better direction for research than trying to find fixed codes.

Paul Read: It may help if we bear in mind the fact that these colours had *names*, names given by the manufacturer. We can probably even identify these particular colours on the nitrate - though not on safety copies. I have, for example, a list of seventeen colours dating from 1918, six years after this film was made, and there's quite clearly a 'referential' element in some of these names: Rose Dorée, Peachblow, Afterglow, Firelight, Candleflame, Sunshine, Verdante, Aquagreen, Turquoise, Azure, Nocturne, Purplehaze, Fleur de Lis, Amaranth, Caprice, Inferno, Argent.

Ivo Blom: But there's a purely conventional element there, too: these seventeen colours were used by all the production companies - there's a very well-defined spectrum in tinting and toning, and it's very difficult to equate this with a system of references to some outer world, because you're working within this very limited scale of colour, which actually amounts to a totally different world.

Peter Delpeut: I disagree. The exact names don't matter so much, because these colours - however much there may have been - function on so many different levels. In different contexts the same yellow or orange can give us a sense of sunlight, of love, or have a narrative function. This can change from one shot to the next. And that's what is so fascinating and at the same time so difficult to grasp: that the colours float in this way among so many levels of meaning.

Don McWilliams: Does it help at all to go back to the nitrates, to trace these complex patterns for, say, a given yellow?

Peter Delpeut: Not really, because the same yellow will have faded differently on different prints. On a print kept in a hot attic it will have faded more than on a print kept in a cellar. I don't really agree with Paul Read that the 'original' colours are identifiable.

Tom Gunning: We can obviously only take a very concrete analysis of particular colours so far, but the initial attempt we're making here with THE GREATER LOVE really does help us reflect about what actually happens as we watch the film. The meanings or experiences the colour generates don't proceed mechanically, they don't work like a code. Only in a few very special cases, like blue-for-night, do we see the colour and know the meaning right away. So whether you take Heide Schlüpmann's approach - saying the meaning isn't very important - or you look for semantic levels, the key thing is that the colour establishes a kind of dialogue with the film as we watch it. We suddenly see the colour through the narrative, or the narrative through the colour, and not just the narrative, but the action, the objects, the people, or the places with non-narrative films. There's a kind of reciprocal process by which these two layers of the film interact, and the dominant element in this interaction is, as Frank Kessler suggested, the *changes* of colour. We know from information theory that if you suddenly switch the means by which you're delivering information everybody's attention sharpens, and if you don't change it the attention level falls. The way colour functions in these films is very much like that, only we have to think not just of attention, but also of involvement, aesthetic response, and so on. Each time we see a new colour, we begin to see the world of the film differently. This sharpening of intensity is perhaps the only intention we can be really sure of in the colouring: the filmmakers wanted to suddenly grab our attention in a new way at that precise moment and with that colour. The meaning or experience this produces is something which only develops as we watch the sequence evolve. And it does develop. We may initially associate the pink with sunset, then associate it with a love affair, then with jealousy, and perhaps finally associate it with nothing in particular, and just have Heide Schlüpmann's sense of a 'pink scene'. But the pinkness is constantly evolving in relation to what we're seeing 'through' it. Our sense of the colour changes as our sense of the scene changes, and vice-versa, and it's precisely this sort of interaction of the two layers that best describes what's really going on.

Daan Hertogs: What part do intertitles play in this sort of development? Because often in a monochrome sequence the intertitles are a different colour. If the colour of the sequence returns after the title - and this perhaps relates to what

Frieda Grafe said about the new impulse given to colour-as-experience by early cinema - you then perhaps have to re-establish the relation between what you're seeing and feeling.

Tom Gunning: That emphasizes something Eric de Kuyper pointed out about the discontinuity in these early films. Intertitles go out of favour in the twenties, with a feeling that pure film shouldn't need them. Here they function on a narrative level, but the colours also draw attention to the distinction between word and image. In this early period, there's a tremendous interest in variety, in constantly giving the audience something new, so that even in a continuous story, there's a 'newness' of colour.

It's quite striking in this film how the colour creates, as both Frank Kessler and Peter Delpeut pointed out, a kind of dramatic continuity, how it seems to be ruled by a kind of narrative structure, as much as anything else. But of course, even if it does play that central role, there's still the interplay between colour and action, and between colour and emotion.

Mariann Lewinsky: When we talk, like Peter Delpeut, about the polyvalent functioning of colour, perhaps we should consider not only the plurality of meaning and function in particular colours, but also the overall effect of the film on the audience. There may be an awful lot going on, constant switching between multiple references and metaphors, but I also get a good overall feeling from these films, from all this variety, including the variety of colour.

Peter Delpeut: When I said at the close of the second session that people who watched these films were intelligent, I meant precisely that they could grasp all these things going on in the films.

Mariann Lewinsky: But it's not just an intellectual grasp - people like to be stimulated through all their senses, and this is exactly what these films give you. That's why I enjoy them so much.

Hans-Michael Bock: I'd like to stress the point that Tom Gunning just made, by suggesting we forget for a moment all the meanings and references and so on, and look at the colours in this film like different typefaces in the film text. You might see the yellow, the black-and-white, the blue, as the standard type. Then in the sequence where the conflict suddenly surfaces for the first time the filmmakers stress this by putting it in Bold, or Italics or something like that. They use a colour that is not used in other parts to stress that something important is happening.

Heide Schlüpmann: It's clear from earlier sessions that we don't really know how the colour got into these films, that we don't know enough about the production process - whether there were colour indications in the scripts, or the colour was decided by the producer or distributor, and so on. We lack the knowledge, the concepts, and the language to address this question of early colour properly. Frieda Grafe pointed out that there's a new kind of colour in these films, but we borrow the language and concepts of our discussion from other fields. A great deal has been written about colour in various fields, but almost no specific language and very few specific concepts have been developed to discuss colour in film. We have to develop new ways to talk about this new sort of colour.

Nicholas Hiley: I'm not very happy with the idea of searching for a code which relates specifically to cinematic colour, or with the idea that these colours have fixed emotional meanings, and names which indicate those meanings. If we go down that path, we're likely to concentrate our attention on fiction films, and on those fiction films where such rules seem to work. We'll end up concentrating - and this has already happened in the study of early film - on areas which seem to have rules, forgetting they don't work for the rest of the cinema programme. The cinema of attractions, for instance, is still represented by newsreels and cine-magazines in twenties film-programmes, but colour-codes do not operate in newsreels. So a twenties audience's memory of lilac isn't a simple memory of lilac. Our basic starting-point should be the fact that the colours *change* in a film. Going back to Tom Gunning's point, what we're really discussing here is the way changes in the films are signalled by changes in the colours. My basic feeling about colour is that it alerts the audience to some change in the film, with the suggestion that we should look for what that change is. It may be a change or new direction in the plot, it might be a new emotional intensity or emphasis, it might be a diegetic change, it might be a change from natural to artificial light. You're being asked to look for some change. If you think about this from the viewpoint of a filmmaker or film manufacturer trying to control changes experienced by an audience, it parallels what the manufacturers were doing with the music in the teens, sending out scores, trying to control the emotions of the audience. These colour changes might also in fact have served as an indication to accompanists that a change was taking place in the film. It's the boundary between colours which is of paramount importance for me as I watch these films. Sometimes a colour change will have a specific emotional or diegetic meaning, but often it won't, it will be signalling some other change - that you've reached the close of one part of the plot and the opening of another. It might also constitute an attempt to control rather unruly audiences receiving films in their own way - here again, the change to sending out music, musical cues, is a better model than some code to be broken, which I just don't think is actually there.

William Uricchio: We haven't yet mentioned contemporary theories of colour: how colour was conceived at the turn of the century, especially ideas about synaesthesia, the blending of sound and image. Some theorists of the period actually linked certain musical motifs with certain colours, certain keys with certain colours, certain chords and certain colours. This parallels the link Nicholas Hiley suggested between colour and music. Maybe we should explore these links between contemporary colour theory and music theory. This broadly echoes Tom Gunning's point that the effect, whether startling or soothing effect or whatever, is the important thing. You might find five or six different codes in a long yellow scene; there's a lot of latitude in possible interpretations, there's a tremendous instability in all the different registers, whether we talk in general terms of movement, or more specifically in terms of emotional prompts or whatever. Maybe we have to broaden the framework current cinema theory with these other discourses.

Sabine Lenk: I want to talk about colour as a kind of attraction, because colour was always a very important factor in selling these films. Cinema owners had to pay more for coloured films. In a standard programme of black-and-white and coloured films it was the coloured films that mattered.

In shorter films - comedies or even dramas - there was lots of action, which people liked. In slightly longer films containing more narrative, perhaps you had to add something to the slow narration, because it was the same audience, accustomed to some kind of attraction. Maybe this explains the colour. In the documentaries shown here, we were amazed by the way the colours stress the beauty of the landscape. In the fiction films the action is much more important than the scenery. THE GOOD PROVIDER had a very long sequence in one colour, then suddenly a second colour right at the end, which creates a real emotion. Then in the film we've been discussing, THE GREATER LOVE, the repeated shock of the colour is often so violent that this must have been a selling-point, an additional attraction.

Eric de Kuyper: Returning to Nicholas Hiley's suggestion about colour as a musical cue, I think it might sometimes have functioned like this, but not generally. I'm thinking of a sequence with five or six shots, each in a totally different colour. How could a pianist possibly follow such 'cues'? It's always a very 'disorderly order' we find in the use of colour.

Nico de Klerk: Any of these patterns - there's action so there's no colour, the link with the music, and so on - work up to a point, but always break down eventually. There are so many different factors at work. Sabine Lenk is of course right up to a point, but then other factors come in, the film programme for example: the colours and other elements of different films in the same programme - locations, actors, and all the rest - all interact in the viewer's memory. There are so many elements in play that any code is bound to break down. And for the same reason, any effort by a production company to control the emotions or the responses of an audience is also bound to break down, it's just too complicated - though perhaps it became possible in the late twenties and early thirties as the programme format started to change and sound was introduced.

Ine van Dooren: As for intertextual memory - some of the contemporary fan magazines have illustrations whose colours seem to follow the typical colouring of fiction films in the teens and twenties, and maybe the two colour systems are linked: they seem to share an identical sort of texture. The same blues, greens and so on.

Peter Delpeut: Eric de Kuyper's final remark summarizes what fascinates me in all this: it's such a disorderly order. And what fascinates me still more is that a spectator has the ability to survive in this disorderly order.

SESSION 6
On Colour Preservation

Mark-Paul Meyer: This session will examine technical aspects of preserving coloured nitrate material on safety stock. Three specialists - Noël Desmet, Mario Musumeci, and Nicola Mazzanti - will show us specimen restorations of their archives and outline the methods used in their laboratories and what they can offer archivists, programmers, and film historians. But first I will ask Paul Read, consultant to a commercial laboratory in London, to open the session with a brief survey of the technical history of applied colour, and of current preservation and restoration methods.

Paul Read: Broadly speaking, from 1895 there were continuing attempts to produce what was often called 'natural' colour - what we would now call 'photographic' colour - by creating in the camera an image of the 'real' colours of a filmed scene. This was, as a whole, commercially and qualitatively unsuccessful until the mid-thirties. There were in fact occasional qualitative successes, like THE TOLL OF THE SEA[1] praised for its 'natural colour', but these exceptions were themselves commercial failures. So an alternative approach was adopted - that of painting or otherwise applying colour onto black-and-white film.

1. Evening Programme, Friday 28 July: THE TOLL OF THE SEA

Several different systems were developed. A toning system - using copper, gold, or uranium baths, had existed for many years prior to motion pictures in the production of paper prints of photographs. This technique was more or less directly plug-in-able to the processing of continuous celluloid film. Stencilling - a development of silkscreen printing - was also quickly adapted to the new medium. Silkscreen printing was itself tried in the early days, and there are patents for silk-screen printing on 35mm and wider formats. Then there were other possibilities such as hand-colouring. It is generally thought that the first technique to be used commercially was toning, although this was probably not the first technique investigated. Tinting, finally, was unique to the motion picture industry. There appears to be no direct parallel in any other medium.

'Natural' colour was already available in still photography by 1895, though not very widely; the printing industry was producing chromolithographs using the conventional subtractive system of multiple plates. So it's not as though the motion picture industry didn't know what it was trying to achieve. It repeatedly attempted to adapt chromolithographic processes, both subtractive and additive[2], to produce good-quality photographic colour. But this was very unsuccessful, in terms of producing successive coloured frames on a commercial basis - that didn't really happen until late in the twenties.

2. Additive colouring processes combine multiple coloured images on the screen, while subtractive processes combine the images on the film print

If you look at the early literature on the development of additive processes, you see there were many experiments, but none was successful. In this literature you'll find technicians sneering at the motion picture industry for using low quality alternatives like tinting and toning. The technical people weren't really interested in what was actually being done. There are no patents for tinting and toning; they're all for developments toward colour photography, pure and simple.

The stencil system reached a peak in the mid-twenties then went downhill very fast. Later stencils are of very poor quality compared with those of the mid-twenties. This had something to do with the economics of a labour-intensive process, and it may well be that stencilling vanished because it was forced out economically. But that takes us beyond the technical history.

One extremely interesting aspect of colour history is the apparent gap where colour vanished, leaving a black-and-white world. There does indeed appear to be such a gap, but there are no obvious technical reasons for it. Somewhere around 1930 sound came in, but there's no technical incompatibility between sound and stencil, tinting, or toning systems. Toned materials actually behave extremely well in terms of optical sound. With tinting you just have to use a different dye, and in 1929 Eastman-Kodak among other manufacturers introduced a range of pre-tinted materials - which Eastman called Sonochrome - specifically for sound film. But these products were taken off the market after just two years. It's only around 1950, with the introduction of the first colour negative materials, that we start to get large numbers of feature films made in colour.

There's a fundamental distinction between applied colour - colour added 'artificially' in accordance with specific decisions in the processing phase - and 'natural' colour predetermined by photographic technology in accordance with a certain 'colour philosophy' before the film is exposed. During the course of the discussion several people have talked about panchromatic and orthochromatic material. There certainly are differences between the way in which various stocks respond to tinting and toning. But nobody, of course, makes film stock today with a view to it being tinted or toned. Panchromatic materials, which are sensitive to all the colours of the spectrum, were first produced in the twenties and are still being made today, while orthochromatic material, sensitive to just green and blue, was discontinued in the sixties. So there's a huge overlap of around forty years when both were being used, and many of us find it difficult, even though we're used to looking at film, to tell whether something was shot on orthochromatic or panchromatic stock. The differences are really quite subtle, since there's a smooth curve of light sensitivity with orthochrome, rather than a sharp cut-off at some point in the spectrum.

We're all constantly investigating how to reproduce the sort of results produced by these old techniques. We're still some way from that goal - there's simply no mechanical way of taking a piece of film and exactly reproducing the colour. We can get very close, often at great expense, but we cannot make a facsimile copy. A better line of research is probably to try and reconstruct the old techniques, and literally reproduce the colour in that sense. But that's not going to be easy and it will take quite some time. We're working with modern materials, which have been developed for quite different purposes. The materials used in the film industry today are not designed for restoring archival film but for something completely different, and we have to twist and turn them to adapt them to this archival job. It's going to take some time to get back to the old technology, but that is our fundamental aim.

There are basically four different ways to reproduce any coloured film. First, you can re-film it on colour negative material, and then make a new colour print. This colour-internegative technique, or direct photographic reproduction, is the standard method in most archives and is the method currently used by the Nederlands Filmmuseum. The problem with this approach is that you're simply copying the present state of the colours, after various degrees of fading. You don't get any sense of the saturation that might have been there originally.

A second approach is to try and reproduce the original saturation. One technique uses colour film as the print stock. If you expose the nitrate to a black-and-white negative, you can either print a black-and-white image or a monochrome image of any colour you like by using filters in the printer - this is effectively a form of toning. You can also directly expose the nitrate film to colour reversal stock, without using a negative at all, and get whatever colours are possible with the three dyes in the printstock, but this is of course limited by the nature of the dyes available in the final print stock. This approach is relatively inexpensive and can be extremely flexible. The problem here is that somebody has to tell the technicians what colour they want.

The third method is to transfer the nitrate image onto digital tape and then manipulate the signal. You can do that either in a framestore, taking as long as you like, which is very expensive, or you can do it in real time, as you transfer the image onto the tape, which severely limits your range of intervention. In either case, with the tape in the form you want, you still have the problem that somebody has to tell the technicians how the colours should be printed. They then take it back out onto a piece of colour negative and make a print, so that you're back on film again.

The fourth method is to go back to the original technology and make a duplicate black-and-white negative from your material. You can then make a print which you can tint or tone using the same technology that was used to colour the original material, but the chance of being able to do that properly is very remote, because you're using modern materials. Yet this is something we should all attempt, if only to better understand the archival material and the old techniques.

Mark-Paul Meyer: This imitation or simulation of the old techniques is used in the Prague archive. They've succeeded in tinting and even toning films the old-fashioned way, using black-and-white stock which is immersed in a dye or chemical bath. I recently saw an example of their work, and it comes very close to what you see on nitrate, though there were problems with that particular print. It's very difficult to get the same density of colour over a whole sequence. They've developed a way of tinting a film without making splices by dipping the entire film, but then the changes of colour are sometimes a little inaccurate. This technique is also very difficult and messy, but Noël Desmet from the archive in Brussels has developed a simple alternative method for tinting and toning, which he will now outline, and which has now been adopted by various other laboratories.

Noël Desmet: This technique was developed at the request of Jacques Ledoux, the former head of my archive. He asked me to find a way to preserve colours, preserve the image, that wasn't too expensive, since then as now there were very limited funds available. This meant I couldn't use expensive colour internegative stock, and had to rely on black-and-white negative material, but I'd already been thinking about the way newspapers used colour-separation, and wondering whether one could apply this to film. Ledoux was very strict about getting as close as possible to the original, and wasn't easily satisfied.

We first make a black-and-white internegative on panchromatic stock that is sensitive to all the colours on the nitrate. This black-and-white negative is then collated with the original on a viewing table in order to get the right colours in the right places. I reconstruct the colours of the original at the viewing table by using three strips - magenta, cyan and yellow. This takes quite a lot of adjustment, and you need the right contrast and density on the negative to get a good match. With relatively low contrast you can manipulate the process more easily.

Normally, you run print stock through a printer and expose it with white light. Of course, you can also expose it with light that has a certain colour temperature, for which you've worked out the gradations. In essence you can choose any colour. So, if you want a toned image, you expose the positive stock through the negative with the desired coloured light, but if you want a tinted image, you directly flash the positive print. If you want a combination of both, you expose right through the negative to get your toned image, then flash the whole positive image for your tint. This involves further separating the nitrate colour into tinted and toned components, which isn't easy, but comes with experience.

The actual colouring decisions are not my responsibility, but are made by an archivist or historian. These decisions are very difficult. I could show you dozens of different types of, say, blue toning with a black-and-white internegative. How do you base your decision on the nitrate? First you have to decide how much the colour has faded, then the degree of toning in the original, as the duration of the chemical bath used to affect the character of the result greatly. And the same sort of considerations apply of course to tinting.

Unfortunately, technicians get only one chance to get all this right, because it's too expensive to make correction prints. We're not always completely happy with the result, and you should perhaps bear this in mind as you watch these films, because I'm sure that for certain films it would be possible to make better prints.

Mark-Paul Meyer: Thank you. Mario Musumeci from the archive in Rome will now outline the methods used there.

Mario Musumeci: As an example of our work, I'll take THE LAST DAYS OF POM-PEII[3]. We found three different copies; two were only tinted and toned, but the copy we found in London had stencil in some scenes. For the tinting, we made a dupli-cate black-and-white negative from the original positive print, then made a new positive print on black-and-white

3. GLI ULTIMI GIORNI DI POMPEI / THE LAST DAYS OF POMPEII Italy 1926 Dir. Carmine Gallone, Amleto Palermi

stock, which we tried to colour by immersion in an aniline bath. The technicians used the old techniques and did some preliminary experiments colouring fragments of the film in an ordinary washing machine on a very long cycle. It takes some time to work out the right composition and concentration of the dye, and the right setting for the 'wash'.

For the stencilled sequences of the film we used colour negative stock, but a camera negative rather than an internegative. This is now standard practice at Rome: our laboratory found that camera negative gives softer contrast and a better reproduction of the colours. We've also experimented with Ektachrome to reproduce stencilled sequences. It generally gives a very good result, but there's the problem that, since you're copying directly onto positive material, you don't get a negative.

In general, we try whenever possible to use black-and-white rather than colour negative stock for preservation since colour negative fades; another problem with the Kodak internegative stock is that it's very difficult to reproduce the typical stencil colours.

Mark-Paul Meyer: I'll now ask Nicola Mazzanti from Bologna to say something about his experience in the archive, where he formerly worked, and their laboratory, where he now works.

Nicola Mazzanti: My experience may help link the work of laboratories and archives, duplication and restoration. Laboratories supply films, documents, for scholars and historians to look at and theorize about. I'd also like to try and link this discussion to what you've actually been seeing on the screen, and the question of why we're so desperate to get as close as possible to the original colour.

I'm acting as a sort of 'intermediary', working in a sort of 'intermediate' laboratory, somewhere between a commercial laboratory and an archive. The laboratory was set up by the archive, which needed somewhere they could get good preservation work done. It was set up by people like myself who had worked for many years in an archive, and then suddenly found themselves on the other side of the fence. Our aim with coloured silent material was to find a preservation technique that was cheap and could be applied systematically on a large scale to produce results as close as possible to the original material. The key thing is to find a method that doesn't restrict the range of colour choices in the future. That's why we have opted for the Desmet method, because when you produce an internegative your interpretation of archival material and the resulting choices will probably determine the appearance of the film in the future, unless some other researcher goes back to the nitrate again in the next twenty or thirty years.

Let me give you some idea of the sort of interpretations and choices we regularly make. You may have the original camera negative of an Italian silent film, with colours indicated on the edges - say, *giallo*, yellow, for scene number ten. Suppose there's no positive nitrate print, then you must yourself choose *what particular yellow* to use. Or you may have a coloured positive print on which the colour indications written on the original negative have been printed onto the positive. And this information may then contradict the colours you actually see on the positive. Or take the specific case of Murnau's NOSFERATU[4]. We had materials from a number of different sources. Most of this material was in black-and-white, but we also had an incomplete coloured print. There must have been a colour change in one scene where the wind blows out the light - the scene would have to become blue. We only had this scene in black-and-white, but we could see where the colour should change, because you could detect on this print where there had been splices in an earlier coloured positive, joining two pieces of nitrate, yellow and blue.

4. NOSFERATU Germany (Prana-Film) 1921

Mark-Paul Meyer: Thank you. Now I would like to invite the rest of you to react to what's been said here.

Stephen Bottomore: When Paul Read says that there was no successful 'natural' colour system until the thirties, I wonder how he measures success, technically and commercially. There were in fact two systems that were fairly successful in both senses. Chronochrome was certainly rather successful technically - it gave a fairly good representation of the real world, if that's how you define technical success. People were absolutely astounded when it was first demonstrated in Britain in 1913. Kinemacolor was perhaps slightly less successful technically, being a two-colour system which couldn't fully reproduce trichromatic human vision. So there were bound to be technical limitations, but there were Kinemacolor branches all over Britain, all over the world - in India, Japan, the United States, France - and quite a lot of them were commercially successful, for a while at least.

When he says toning was the first colour system he may be right, I just don't know. We could say the same about a whole lot of questions that have been asked these last few days, we just don't know. My own research actually indicates that hand-colouring was the first colour process. I have about fifteen names of people who were hand-colouring in the first ten or fifteen years of cinema, and that's just the tip of the iceberg, there were a whole lot more - fairground people, wives and daughters of filmmakers, and so on.

As for stencilled colour reaching its peak in the mid-twenties - are we talking here about a qualitative or quantitative peak, the most extensive use of stencilling or the most perfect stencil colouring? I just don't know: I've never seen any statistical study of this.

I'd also like to question what seems to be the general consensus here that there's not much about colour in the contemporary literature. In the trade press, at least, there are hundreds of articles relating to the history of colouring, quite often at variance with more recent histories. Let me, for example, contrast contemporary accounts with our discussion here of toning. You read in the contemporary literature how the chemicals used were highly poisonous, caused numerous deaths in darkrooms and so on, in the nineteenth century. Does that have any bearing on the history of toning films? Might it have discouraged people from using this process, or didn't they care? How many people died toning films? Again, we just don't know. Another interesting thing you find in contemporary sources but not in more recent accounts is that you could actually tone films without any chemicals at all. Articles from 1909 describe how by altering the exposure of the print - usually by increasing it massively, with up to ten times the normal amount of light going on to the print - and reducing the concentration of the developer, again massively, then balancing these factors, you could create quite a good range of colours from dark brown and sepia through to purple and dark red. It would be interesting to look for evidence of this process in the prints that have come down to us. And there are all sorts of other things relating to hand colouring and stencilling which you won't find in the text books, but about which you find interesting details in contemporary articles.

Mark-Paul Meyer: To reply to your question about stencilling in the twenties, from my experience in the archive, stencils from the twenties can be of a really perfect quality, and really look like photographic colour. It's also clear that some companies do it better than others. THE GLORIOUS WEST COUNTRY[5], for instance, is a British stencilling that isn't as good - or perfect - as most Pathé stencilling from 1923 or 1924.   5. Session 2

Ine van Dooren: We've talked a lot here about the experience of colour in screen projection. But when we talk about reproducing the colours and this expe- rience, we should also bear in mind that silent cinema used lighting systems and screens that were quite different from those we use today.

Paul Read: There's one place in the world where it has hardly changed - India. They're still using carbon arcs, and stretched and painted cotton screens. They grade or balance the films for the slightly greenish light you get with carbon arcs. These prints can't actually be used in Europe, because with our projection systems they look too red, too warm, and a separate batch of prints has to be produced for distribution outside India.

Daan Hertogs: Let me try and focus the discussion by asking a very general question. If the technicians from the lab come to us saying, 'We can do anything you want, get any colour under the sun', what actually is it that we want as film programmers, scholars, archivists, makers, from preservation?

Mark-Paul Meyer: I want, as an archivist, to be able to tell them exactly what I want, but the problem is that I often just don't know, just don't have enough information for a really confident decision about the original colours of the nitrate. Recently, for instance, we restored QUO VADIS[6], which had sequences in beautiful tinting and toning in the third and   6. QUO VADIS Italy (Cines) 1912/3 fourth reels. But in the last reel, I could see that these   Dir. Enrico Guazzoni] beautiful tinting and toning scenes were actually decayed. Using a black-and-white duplicate negative we can restore any amount of blue toning and pink tinting, but I really needed more information about how films decay. If I knew more about how blue toning turns brown, or pink toning turns yellow, I would have been in a better position to ask the technicians to print scenes in certain blues and pinks, rather than simply duplicating the nitrate on a colour internegative and getting what looks like - beautiful - brown toning and yellow tinting.

I'd like to have a huge database of different colours and different techniques. We do have some original Pathé catalogues and Agfa colour-cards, but there's a lot more of this stuff. If you had a systematic catalogue you might be able to name a colour on, say, a Kodak print of 1923, from what you knew about the colours then available and how they were used. This is related to another huge problem for archives: no colours last forever, not even in the preservation prints we make, so we're desperately looking for a method, a system, to describe colours. There are scientific ways to do this, with a densitometer and spectrometer, but it's very time-consuming; maybe we'll think of some faster method to identify colours. Maybe the technicians or archivists themselves should start to work in this direction.

Enno Patalas: I also have wondered how to judge from the actual state of colours on nitrate prints what they were originally. Sometimes you can get very valuable information about the original state of the colours from the frames cut out by contemporary projectionists when they were splicing together the reels. A Munich collector has an album of such frames, which we used when restoring THE CABINET OF DR. CALIGARI[7]. He had about thirty perfectly preserved frames from various parts of the film. From the badly decayed Montevideo print we could identify the colour changes, and from the Munich album we could see what the colours originally looked like. I wonder whether scientists could tell us whether colours always decay the way these colours decayed, whether there's any pattern in the decay?

7. DAS KABINETT DES DR. CALIGARI /
THE CABINET OF DR. CALIGARI,
Germany (Decla) 1919
Dir. Robert Wiene

Paul Read: Given unlimited funds we could, in principle, identify almost all the dyes and tone-colours in a piece of film, even if they were to some extent degraded or decayed. There are several chemical techniques for doing this. The problem is that although we know a great deal about the different systems that were used and their chemistry, nobody has yet sat down to work out a catalogue or database of colours and patterns of decay that could be used to identify the original colours. Quite a number of archives are currently considering whether to fund this type of research. But it's still unclear exactly how much such a programme would cost. One part of the problem is that around two hundred different commercial colour systems have been used and it's actually very difficult to identify them. Just to complicate matters, various people have estimated that even where the colour-system is noted on an archival copy, 80% of such labelling is inaccurate. Chemical analysis of the dyes may actually be the only way to systematically identify the process used. We currently rely mainly on the edge-markings, the gauge and similar factors for identification.

Erik de Kuyper: Mark-Paul Meyer talked about the beauty of decay in QUO VADIS. I'm all for restoration and trying to get back the original image - at great risk, it's a very risky game to play. At the same time, since we're currently doing so much preservation and restoration, it would also be good to have a kind of image of the decay itself, like a sort of photograph of the film before restoration. Most of the nitrate is disappearing and it would be good to have a few interesting specimens of what it was like in decay. This may seem a little perverse, it may be a question of taste; but this taste for decay is itself an element of our culture, which we can't really ignore, because restoration too is a matter of taste as well as technology. Any restoration reflects some ideology, however unconscious, associated with a certain historical taste. The coming generation might want to have these patterns of decay as well as wonderful restorations and preservations - a systematic collection of relics or records - maybe just photographs - of the interesting state of decay of early film at the end of this century. The paper-print collection at the Library of Congress has turned out to be very useful. Maybe later generations will have a use for this sort of perversion I'm advocating. Maybe they will have new and better methods of reconstructing early films, and be able to use these records, these ruins, when all our nitrates have disappeared.

Tom Gunning: What we're always seeking, in a way, is a dialogue with the past. We obviously use all our techniques of research and reconstruction to try and define that past. But we must always remain aware of the gap that separates it from us, and the need to keep both points - the past and the present - in focus in order to pursue a real dialogue. We can't, in other words, just hold up a mirror to the past, we must in some sense engage it. It's a very exciting idea to recreate the whole context of silent film: to have the 'original' music, the theatre, the projection. But we must realize this is an impossible ideal: the audience will be totally different; as soon as you walk out of the theatre it's totally different; the mindset we bring into the theatre is totally different. That's only a problem if we think we're trying to mirror or totally recreate the past, which is of course impossible. Our goal should rather be a dialogue, not only with a film on the screen, but with a number of elements of its presentation and context, and it's always good to extend the range of that dialogue. But it's also important to see silent films with scores written in the 1990s - accompanied by pianists with modern sensibilities - to preserve our sense of distance. What would the nineteenth century have been without its taste for ruins? Our sense of architecture, of history, of the past is partly shaped by a nineteenth-century fascination not just with reconstructions but with ruins. And although it's very important to recognize the tragedy of so much of our film history lying in ruins, these ruins in themselves have a certain fascination of their own, a certain reality that's worth saving even while we lament it.

Nicolas Hiley warned us in Session 3 never to forget the economic factors in the history of colour. And what clearly seems to rule so many of the decisions in archival preservation is economics. I'm not suggesting any alternative, but we should never forget, either, how amazingly marginal our societies have made this task of preservation. It's expensive, but compared with many other projects undertaken by various governments and world organizations, it's not that expensive. The fact that so many possibilities and projects discussed here remain just possibilities and projects, that we can't even get successive prints, but usually have to make do with an answer print, obviously reflects economic decisions by larger forces than ourselves, shows us our marginality, and suggests this work will always be underfunded. Hopefully there is some way that as educators and so on we might work to change that.

Péter Forgács: The fact that an archive doesn't have enough money to make a second or third print makes the archivist rather like a filmmaker working with found footage - when you touch the material you change it, you put it in a different context.

Nico de Klerk: What exactly are the laboratories trying to achieve in restored prints? With the restoration system used in this archive, it's sometimes impossible to reproduce certain colours, because of the limitations of the colour internegative. In Prague and Brussels, on the other hand, they use black and white stock, so the reproduction of colours is more accurate, but there seems to be a lack of contrast. Is that an inherent disadvantage of these systems, or something specific to these particular films, or is it perhaps because contrast isn't considered very important? There seem to be advantages and disadvantages in each system, and I'd like to hear more about the priorities informing their use.

Daan Hertogs: But surely it's not the technicians who demonstrated these processes that should explain *their* priorities - they're the people who are saying to scholars such as yourself, 'We can do anything, what do *you* want?'

Nico de Klerk: We want a lot, but the Amsterdam archive, for example, always uses the same system, though we know there are certain disadvantages. Can we accept those disadvantages, or do we want to get round them?

Peter Delpeut: We work mainly with the Haghefilm method for one important reason. If you want to process 5,000 meters a week, then this system is a very good choice. We've been discussing colour and preservation methods ever since I arrived at the archive. We've sent test strips to Prague, Bologna, and other archives for processing, and all the results were quite interesting, but their methods can't be applied on the same scale - you just can't use them to process 5,000 meters a week. That doesn't mean we're not constantly exploring all sorts of different approaches.

Daan Hertogs: Since we have to work with safety stock and aren't allowed to show nitrate, you'll get a different dialogue with the past in Brussels and in Amsterdam, where the acetates are produced by different methods. Is it a problem that you then have, in a sense, two different films?

Tom Gunning: It would be a problem if you didn't understand the difference. One important contribution of this Workshop is precisely to have explained that difference to film scholars. Many of us may have known beforehand that there were different ways to preserve colour, but we didn't know they produced different results. It's important in a dialogue to know the different vocabularies available. Only then can we start to establish priorities - not by examining our conscience, but as we converse and interact with the past and each other. My appreciation of the Desmet and Prague methods - seeing those blacks underneath the colour - isn't just a question of liking the result, but derives also from our conversations here about the role of colour in silent film as a kind of superadded quality, as something more than simply an attempt at naturalism. The discussion here inclines me, in general, to prefer the Desmet method, but I'm only just beginning to understand the differences, and it's too early to reach any firm conclusions.

Enno Patalas: People think a lot about what to do with the extant archival material, but nobody seems to think very much about all the material that's missing. When footage, intertitles, and so on are missing, people still 'restore' the film in the way you might restore a chair to look as if it had been made yesterday - so you can sit in it comfortably. This isn't the right way to preserve furniture or film, removing all traces of the past, of its distance, of the decay. We shouldn't try to make these relics more comfortable, nicer; we should try to become more conscious of their distance from us, and what's missing, in particular.

Don McWilliams: It seems there are two types of dialogue with the past. Making a film with some restored footage is an attempt to have a dialogue with the past on its own terms, to enter into that past. But unrestored footage and photographs are sometimes in such a bad state you can hardly make out the image. We can restore, enhance, that image, or we can use it as we find it - torn photographs, imperfect fixatives, faded old footage with all the scratches and even bits of the frame missing - and this is to bring the past into the present, to make the connection with mortality. Despite all the decay, the gestures and all the other things we share with the past are there in front of us, not cleaned up, but showing the passage of time. That's what I always find most moving, and what I most want to put into my films, and transmit to modern viewers.

Nicola Mazzanti: Our job is basically to transform nitrate films into something else, to try and restore a soul to a dead body. We're simply not allowed to project nitrates so we create something else, an acetate projection print. One major concern is to define principles that should guide this tranformation. With colour in silent film we seem to be on the point of passing from a period of experimentation to a certain number of standards, which are now basically settled for each different method. This implies that we must now begin to establish fixed methodologies for duplication at least, if not for restoration. But how many laboratories, how many archivists and scholars, are ready to meet these standards? Once this has been done, we can face the real challenge, which is the sound and colour of the fifties and sixties.

Nicholas Hiley: We're placing a very heavy responsibility on archivists, asking them to make a lot of decisions which are clearly very difficult. This reflects a tendency that has surfaced a number of times over the past few days, to believe that we can somehow stand outside time, that somehow the decisions we make won't change the historical record, won't in fact change history in any way. You often see this at conferences and among film historians - the idea that we watch these films without being an audience, that these films don't embody any creative decisions, aren't produced by 'film-makers'. I find it reassuring to realize that we are an audience, and that archivists are filmmakers. Any process of preservation involves creative decisions. We scholars have a relationship with archivists and technicians that exactly mirrors the film industry: we're consumers and the archivists are producers. And what happens in such a relationship is that you always get the cheapest possible solution the audience will tolerate. And the audience has to make decisions too. We're offered a whole range of choices, and we have to say what we want, and what we're prepared to pay for. I'm quite happy with this, I like audiences, I like being an audience, and I think the decisions they make are usually the right ones. I'm not quite sure why we should be trying to deny we're in this sort of relationship with archivists and technicians, and to abdicate all our responsibility for these decisions.

PART II:

COLOURED IMAGES TODAY:
HOW TO LIVE WITH SIMULATED COLOURS
(A N D   B E   H A P P Y)

by Giovanna Fossati

I.

During the Workshop sessions a ghost was floating in the air, the ghost of the nitrate print. The films were of course projected in acetate prints, but from the very first day it became clear to everybody that the prints screened were quite different from the nitrate that remained on the shelves in the archive. In the final session a number of technicians outlined the problems involved in making the sort of prints we were watching, explaining the choices and possibilities in making acetate projection prints from coloured nitrate prints[1] and the quite different results the range of options offers. Thus one thing that became apparent over the course of the Workshop was the need for a theoretical approach to colour preservation. Such theorizing is a concern of all the parties involved: technicians, archivists, scholars, indeed anyone else who cares about the preservation of our film heritage. Let us try to face the problem and see if we can exorcise the ghost of the nitrate.

1. Originally, of course, nitrate prints were projection prints as well, but they cannot be projected any longer. In fact, projection of nitrate prints is legally prohibited.

In the literature on film preservation it is not uncommon to find coloured nitrate prints compared to paintings. Up to a certain point such a comparison is valid. In the first place, both paintings and coloured nitrates are objects that have been painted, they both 'carry' the colours that were originally applied. The aniline dyes[2] we find on a nitrate print today are the dyes that were applied directly to that print: no matter how many prints were made of a film, each print was coloured individually. Secondly, both the pigments on a painting and the dyes on a film print change over time. The aniline dyes have faded progressively through repeated exposure to the heat of the projector's lamp, they have undergone chemical reactions with the film's emulsion, they have decayed, sometimes they have completely disappeared; in short, the colours have changed and are still changing.

2. Aniline dyes are transparent chemical dyes available in a range of colours, whose production began during the second half of the last century. The tints were used to colour lantern slides before being used to colour films.

Faced with the task of preservation, the art-restorer and the film-restorer, confronting their respective objects, will each presumably do all they can to let the object and its colours live longer.

From this point on the comparison starts to break down. In a painting the colours actually *are* the image while with a coloured nitrate the photographic image is both conceptually and physically distinct from the colours applied upon it. And when the parallel between art-preservation and film-preservation is taken a step further to the level of actual restoration, an essential difference between the two activities becomes apparent. By 'preservation' I here intend the very broad conception of restoring an art object to a condition that it can be exhibited again. The art-restorer, confronted with a painting, will work on the object itself. The film-restorer, on the other hand, apart from repairing splices and perforations, will not work on the object - the nitrate print - but will have a new copy made. Only this acetate projection print will then be exhibited. Once a nitrate print has disappeared (nitrate film deteriorates at a much faster rate than paintings), all that remains is this projection print. Thus the painting's material is restored in a reversible way - at least in principle - that allows one to distinguish what was there before the restoration and what has been added or changed. The film, on the other hand, is made visible only by making *another* print. No reversibility is involved.

Making a copy, a projection print, while leaving the coloured nitrate basically untouched is, one could say, a radical intervention compared to the way paintings are restored. It is also in a sense more radical than the preservation of black-and-white nitrate prints. In the preservation of colour and black-and-white nitrate films, projection prints are struck on a different kind of film stock than was used for the original. Projection prints made today, even of black-and-white films, have a different visual quality from the nitrate prints.[3] The manufacture of a black-and-white print involves the effect of light on photographic material. From the silent period down to the present day this principle has remained constant. But the technologies once used to colour films are different, in their principles and in practice, from the technology which allows us, today, to make projection prints from coloured nitrates. Coloured nitrate prints were black-and-white prints on the images of which colour was physically applied, while acetate projection prints are colour prints whose colour is produced by a colour emulsion which is there before the image. On a technical level, applied colours were the result of systems (hand - and stencil colouring, tinting and toning) that disappeared from the manufacture of film prints a long time ago, whereas current preservation methods involve a technology used in contemporary cinematography to produce colour by photographic means.[4] Paul Read, in a conversation during the Workshop, aptly called contemporary colour preservation methods 'colour simulation', and from this perspective we might more generally see the preservation of coloured nitrate prints as 'colour simulation': a radical intervention to make a projection print from a coloured nitrate, in which we neither preserve nor restore but 'simulate' the colours.

3. There are of course many further discrepancies beyond those between old and new film stock. There are technical differences in all phases of filmmaking, processing, and projection. Changes in film materials are decided by the industries that produce them, and the main concern of these industries is not to ease the preservation process.

4. There are actually a few preservation methods that imitate the old tinting and toning techniques, but even then the material used is different from that of the silent period.

A question arises immediately from this line of thought: are these projection prints surrogates for the disappearing coloured nitrates? Or to put it more provocatively: are these prints fakes? In a recent article, Paolo Cherchi Usai has empha-sized the fact that colour is the aspect most likely to disappear from moving images. According to him, all we can say about colour is no more than a compromise between a memory and the experience of what is visible today. As far as the silent era is concerned, the experience of colours is based on a loving lie, which we tacit-ly accept. Tinting, toning, hand - and stencil-colouring, and even the first and second Technicolor processes (both involving tinting techniques) are made the same by contemporary laboratory procedures: today's systems cannot render the original systems used to colour the films in the first place. In Cherchi Usai's opi-nion it is pointless to ask which contemporary system is more or less faithful to what it reproduces:

'We should, rather, question the value of discussing them as though we were unaware of the gap between any particular process and the objects it exhumes (...) Can such objects provide the basis for any systematic appreciation? If we are for-ced to assess, not the work itself, but one of its reincarnations (however arbitrary, or however informed by some dominant technology of reproduction), then what constraints does this impose, and what guiding principles, in particular, must we adopt? (...) We must recognize that a contemporary copy of a film radiated an "aura" (in the Benjaminian sense) missing from modern duplicates (...) We simply have to face an unavoidable and cruel choice: to accept an essential "infidelity" inextricably linked with the idea of restoring moving images - and all its metho-dological implications - or (paradoxically?) to continue projecting the nitrate to destruction, recognizing extant prints as their own only valid representatives.[5]

The passage resonates with a strong melancholic mood, a sense of loss. Cherchi Usai suggests that projec-tion prints are unfaithful copies of the nitrate 'originals'. From this point of view, projection prints are conceptual-ly no different from reproductions of paintings. They present us with something in which unfaithfulness is inevitable, with something whose the aura has been lost.

The idea of an 'aura' was of course used by Benjamin to distinguish the traditional arts, with their aura of the unique original, from mechanically reproduced arts in which the unique original no longer figured as a concept or object. But in Cherchi Usai's text film - or rather silent film - appears to have changed sides and become a traditional art. As Tom Gunning said during the Workshop, 'what is interesting now, after another fifty, sixty years of film, is that we approach it as preservatio-nists. We begin to feel there is something rather unique about certain prints, something which ought to be preserved.'[6] Thus the idea of uniqueness *can* in fact be associated in various ways with silent films - with the uniqueness of a film of which no other prints exist, the uniqueness of a print which embodies transformations distinct from those undergone by other prints of the same film, or the uniqueness of a particular print's colours. On this view, a nitrate print becomes rather like a painting. In other words, if the aura of a film lies only in the object, in the nitrate

5. Paolo Cherchi Usai, 'Le nitrate mécanique. L'imagination de la couleur comme science exacte (1830-1928)', in Jacques Aumont (ed.), LA COULEUR EN CINÉMA, Paris - Milan (Cinémathèque Française - Mazzotta) 1995, pp. 104-5

6. Session 1, p. 18

print, it is indeed inevitable that it will disappear with the nitrate. To answer my earlier question from this perspective, considering only the material life of films, projection prints *are* mere surrogates or fakes because they do not preserve the aura of the nitrate.

II.

Why, then, do we make 'another' print when it is clear that it comes nowhere near the materiality of the nitrate? First of all, we seem to have no choice, as before long the nitrate will cease to exist and this other print will be the only one available. Secondly, loss of the original material does not mean that our link with the past will be completely severed - not if we take into account that we can look at film not only as a material object but also as a series of projected images. Such a shift in perspective would mean a shift from the nitrate print to the film performance. This perspective, incidentally, corresponds to developments in film historiography that since the late seventies have produced alternatives to some of the key concepts researchers employed in the study of cinema and that particularly affected the study of early cinema: '[A] shift (...) from the film as text and textual object to the film in performance', as Thomas Elsaesser put it.[7]

7. Session 1, p. 20

In fact, the unique nitrate print, which cannot be projected and remains, therefore, a mere object in a vault, can never be considered the complete film. Only the film performance can establish a film's continuous history. Of course, any reproduction is capable of doing that job, even a magnetic reproduction. There may come a time when a film performance will be an individual experience in front of a monitor - maybe that time has already come.[8] For the moment though, I prefer to pursue the idea of a film performance as an event that includes a theatre and an audience, a projector and a projectionist, a screen and a print that is projected, for the simple but important reason that with the acetate projection print the prevalent early exhibition mode of film is preserved as well.

8. Douglas Gomery liberally defines film exhibition as ranging 'from the simple nickelodeon to the ornate movie palace, from the unpretentious neighborhood theatre to the orchestrated marketing of the multiplex in the shopping mall, from television's repetitive Late Show to vast selections available in the world of home video.' See his SHARED PLEASURES. A HISTORY OF MOVIE PRESENTATION IN THE UNITED STATES, London (BFI) 1992, p. xviii.

If, today, we project a film made in the silent era, we will be projecting an acetate print. Now, if we accept that acetate prints are part of the continuous history of a film rather than mere surrogates, the range of options that is open in making those prints suddenly becomes an issue of immense importance. Archives have conceived, in collaboration with film laboratories, different methods to print coloured nitrate films on acetate film stock. As each method produces different results, results that become part of the film's performance, we clearly need to take a closer look at these methods.

III.

The simulation of colours on a projection print is not an automatic and neutral process. It is not automatic because there is more than one method available; it is not neutral because the choice of the method affects the result that will appear on the projection print. In other words, choosing a method is the final step in an interpretative process. During the Workshop three different methods were discussed in some detail: the colour internegative method, the Desmet method, and the method of imitating the original tinting and toning techniques. The second and the third methods can only be used for tinted and toned films, while the colour internegative method can reproduce stencilled and hand coloured films as well.

A solarized film is a good example of how the choice of methods affects the result. Solarization is a term used for the chromatic disintegrations that show up on a nitrate film, irrespective of whether an entire sequence is affected or just a limited number of frames. A blue tinting that has turned yellow would for instance be called solarization. Now, the colour internegative method is the only method in which solarizations are inevitably copied from the nitrate to the acetate print. To put it more simply, the colour internegative method is like taking a photograph of the nitrate, with all its damage and decay. The Desmet method and the 'imitative' method, on the other hand, do not necessarily have to copy solarizations. To use the same metaphor, these methods are like taking a black-and-white photograph of the nitrate, then adding colour to the image.

We are dealing here with (at least) two different conceptions of a preservation of a coloured film. One aims at the simulation of colours as they were at the moment of preservation. This conception is exemplified by the colour internegative method. The other aims at the simulation of the colours as they appeared on the nitrate print before being affected by projection and the passage of time (fading, solarization and other forms of decay). This conception is exemplified by the Desmet method and the 'imitative' method. While the Desmet method uses an acetate print's colour emulsion, the 'imitative' method in particular reveals a strong desire to recreate exactly what was, or might have been, once there, even to the point of imitating the systems that coloured the prints.

But things, as usual, are more complicated than this. The colour internegative method does not simulate the colours exactly as they now appear on the nitrate print today.[9] And the other two methods cannot actually recreate what was there, because it is not possible to determine accurately how the colours appeared, say, eighty years ago. Thus each method suits a certain conception of preservation only potentially. And as each coloured nitrate poses different problems, my feeling is, rather, that there is no final solution, no particular method that solves all these problems. Each nitrate print or group of prints may inspire different approaches, in both analysis and preservation. When, for instance, the colours function on a narrative level, it may be necessary to undo such traces of time as solarizations or fadings in order to make the narration intelligible. In the NFM print of THE LONEDALE OPERATOR[10], a blue tinting

9. See Session 1 for some of the limitations of the colour internegative method.

10. Session 1: DE MOEDIGE DOCHTER VAN DEN STATIONSCHEF / THE LONEDALE OPERATOR United States (Biograph) 1911 Dir. D.W. Griffith.

has faded in most of the frames of the shot in which the heroine switches off the lights in the room to make the bandits think she is holding a gun in her hand. Without the blue her trick fails - for her adversaries as well as for the audience: instead of a gun she's holding a harmless object - a small monkey wrench - in what is perceived as a fully lit room. To restore narrative comprehension it is necessary here to restore the blue tinting. A different approach is followed with the print of CAP-TAIN F.E. KLEINSCHMIDT'S ARCTIC HUNT[11] a great number of travelogue shots have turned into a strikingly anti-naturalistic, not to say hellish, red. Instead of trying to recreate the colours as they might have been, retaining these solarizations may well add to the beauty of further projections of the film and would not in itself interfere with the intelligibility of the images. It is important then to remain flexible in the preservation of coloured prints.

11. Session 5: IN HET NOORDPOOL-GEBIED / CAPTAIN F.E. KLEIN-SCHMIDT'S ARCTIC HUNT United States 1924 Dir. Frank E. Kleinschmidt.

Something else has to be kept in mind too, which is that preservation methods are constantly being improved, adapted and occasionally even superseded. Digital preservation is already a possibility, but it is still too expensive to be adopted on a large scale. But as soon as this happens, it will necessitate a lot of rethinking in the area of colour preservation. The method is much more flexible than any other method in use today, allowing digital simulation of a much larger range of colours (although the film will suffer a certain loss of colour quality in performance, through the process of transfer to acetate). With the freedom this offers it is evident that one should have a very clear idea of the result one wants to achieve. For that reason it is very important to explicitly state the interpretation that led to the preservation of a certain print in a certain way.

On the other hand, from the researchers' point of view, it is important to be aware of what film restoration can actually achieve. I am not implying that film researchers should have detailed knowledge of the technologies involved in film preservation, as long as they are aware of the range of choices, of how preservation methods affect the film in performance, of what film archives and film laboratories do, and, finally, of the materials used, since even contemporary colour film stock 'already embodies a certain ideology of colour, of certain balances and limits' as Tom Gunning pointed out during the Workshop.[12] It is important to have a clear image of all these factors, because that is the only way to discuss a film performed by the projection print in a critical way.

12. Session 4, p.57

IV.

Writing history, writing the history of colour in cinema, is a work of interpretation of documents, of coloured films. Challenging the positivistic approach of the 1800s, Jacques Le Goff and the Nouvelle Histoire movement stressed that an objective, primary document does not exist. The first goal of an historian is 'to critically discuss a document - any document - as if it were a monument.'[13] For Le Goff

13. This and the following quote are from: Jacques Le Goff, 'Documento/monumento', in: ENCICLOPEDIA, Torino (Einaudi) 1978, pp.38-48, vol. V (my translation, GF).

there is no such thing as an innocent document. Firstly, any such object will have been materially altered by an editing process - as Le Goff calls it - effected by the society and era that produced it. Secondly, it is also an interpretation, 'a product of later eras during which the document lived - or was perhaps forgotten, during which it was retouched - albeit by silence. (...) Document is monument. (...) Taken to its extreme, a document-truth does not exist. Any document is a lie.'

'Document is monument' is a formulation that integrates the history of the object itself (in its material transformations) with the interpretations of the object over time. In terms of film history and the coloured nitrate print, one might say that Le Goff's 'editing process' is the film's production and circulation. To the extent that it is 'a product of later eras', for instance an acetate preservation, things are a bit more complicated. On the one hand, as a performance, the acetate projection print revives a particular film's circulation and creates a new chapter in its history. On the other hand, as a new object, a new piece of film, it is a work of interpretation of that particular film. In the case of nitrate film, such an interpretation is inescapable, since the nitrate has a finite life and can no longer be projected. That interpretation of course will become part of the film's history since it will influence all its further projections.

These observations force us to articulate the approaches followed in the interpretation of coloured prints and their transfer from nitrate to safety stock. Only then are we really in a position to discuss the results. Inevitably then, the film restorer becomes part of the history of the print he or she works on. Like anyone who undertakes historical research on an aesthetic object, his or her limits will be the technological limits of the method chosen. The history of applied colours is written on the projection prints, a history bearing the signs of the time and of the interpretations.

To return to the question posed in my title, I would say that if the life of coloured films does not so much reside in its material but rather in its performative dimension, we should consider the performance of acetate projection prints today as part of the films' lives. We should not feel unhappy in the way we would feel unhappy if we saw them as mere surrogates for what once was there. Depending on our particular point of view - as a scholar, archivist, or spectator - we will look at the simulated colours on a projection print differently, and we will ask different questions. A projection print and its colours can answer any question we may want to ask it. If we ask about all the projections it has been through, it will probably have a lot to say. But if we ask how it originally looked, the answer will probably be a lie.

APPENDIX 1:
Programme Overview

Wednesday 26 July 1995, 17.00 - 18.30

Opening screening:
MODE IN BEWEGING / FASHION IN MOTION / MODE IN BEWEGING
The Netherlands (Nederlands Filmmuseum) 1992 ❖ Compiled by Peter Delpeut &
José Teunissen ❖ DK1560 - 1473m / video 113 - 73' ❖ black-and-white,
tinting, stencil, two-colour Technicolor
Today fashion and motion are closely associated - even in still photographs the
models appear to be sweeping by rather than posing to show the clothes they're
wearing. Fashion is something that should be seen in motion. In fact, it is the
motion picture that revolutionized fashion and its forms of presentation. But, as
the early fashion films of the teens and twenties demonstrate, the ease and
naturalness of the current fashion show began falteringly. The pace is slow and
often uneasy. For the production companies this was no handicap, judging from
the precise and detailed way in which these films were coloured.

Wednesday 26 July 1995, 20.30 - 22.00

Evening screening:
The Evening screenings were devoted mainly to feature films and were meant to
complement the daytime sessions, in which only excerpts of feature-length films
could be shown.

BITS & PIECES 36 - 41 / *idem* / - ❖ DK1393 - 223m / video 298 - 12'
tinting, stencil

HARAKIRI / *idem* / *idem* ❖ Germany (Declafilm) 1919 Dir. Fritz Lang
DK1471 - 1647m ❖ tinting, toning
This *Madame Butterfly* adaptation by Fritz Lang was preserved with the Desmet
method in the laboratory of the Cineteca di Bologna, from a nitrate print of the
Nederlands Filmmuseum.

Thursday 27 July, 9.30 - 12.45
Session 1 - Programme Notes

Thursday 27 July, 14.00 - 17.00
Session 2 - A Colourful Education

Thursday 27 July, 20.30 - 22.00

Evening Programme:
TOKYO DRIFTER / *idem* / TOKYO NAGAREMONO ❖ Japan (Nikkatsu) 1966 Dir. Suzuki Seijun ❖ 83' ❖ colour film
Suzuki Seijun's film seems to revive the freedom colours enjoyed in films from the teens. Here a number of times the photographic colour of the film is 'stretched' to the limits. Notable is the scene of a woman dying, in which the red of the background gets darker and darker.

Friday 28 July, 9.30 - 12.45
Session 3 - A Slippery Topic: Colour as Metaphor, Intention or Attraction?

Friday 28 July, 14.30 - 17.45
Session 4 - What's the Difference?

Friday 28 July, 20.30 - 22.30

Evening Programme:

TOLL OF THE SEA / *idem / idem* ❖ United States (Universal) 1922 Dir. Chester
Franklin ❖ DK1651 - 1164m / video 347 - 58' ❖ two-colour Technicolor
In the twenties a number of two-colour Technicolor feature films were produced,
among which this *Madame Butterfly* adaptation. The film was restored by the
Film Department of U.C.L.A.

THE LAST OF THE MOHICANS / *idem / idem* ❖ United States (Maurice Tourneur
Productions) 1920 Dir. Maurice Tourneur, Clarence Brown ❖ DK828 - 1560m /
video 128 - 76' ❖ tinting
An example of the changing use of tinting in the twenties. Although there is less
variation in colours and the colour changes are not as abrupt as in the teens, numerous sequences in this western show that tinting can still be a stunning effect.

Saturday 29 July, 9.30 - 12.45
Session 5 - Monochromes: Anarchy, but not without Order

Saturday 29 July, 14.30 - 17.30
Session 6 - On Colour Preservation

Saturday 29 July, 20.30 - 22.30

Evening programme:
Open air screening of
THE EPIC OF THE EVEREST / *idem / idem* ❖ Great-Britain 1924, Dir. J.B.L. Noel
D6151 - 1687m ❖ black-and-white, tinting
Sparing but extremely effective use of tinting, turning Mount Everest into a
distant, mysterious goddess.

APPENDIX 1:
List of participants

Richard Abel (Drake University)
Des Moines, United States

Jacques Aumont (Université de Sorbonne Nouvelle)
Paris, France

Ansje van Beusekom (Vrije Universiteit)
Amsterdam, The Netherlands

Ivo Blom (Universiteit van Amsterdam)
Amsterdam, The Netherlands

Hans-Michael Bock (CineGraph)
Hamburg, Germany

Coby Bordewijk (Rijksuniversiteit Leiden)
Leiden, The Netherlands

Stephen Bottomore (researcher, filmmaker)
London, England

Carlos Bustamante (Hochschule der Künste)
Berlin, Germany

Peter Delpeut (filmmaker, Nederlands Filmmuseum)
Amsterdam, The Netherlands

Noël Desmet (Koninklijk Filmarchief/Cinémathèque Royale)
Brussels, Belgium

Karel Dibbets (Universiteit van Amsterdam)
Amsterdam, The Netherlands

Ine van Dooren (South East Film and Video Archive)
Brighton, England

Thomas Elsaesser (Universiteit van Amsterdam)
Amsterdam, The Netherlands

Péter Forgács (filmmaker)
Budapest, Hungary

Annette Förster (Rijksuniversiteit Utrecht)
Utrecht, The Netherlands

Giovanna Fossati (Università di Bologna)
Bologna, Italy

Frieda Grafe (writer, film critic)
Munich, Germany

Karola Gramann (J.W. Goethe Universität)
Frankfurt, Germany

Herman Greven (Nederlands Filmmuseum)
Amsterdam, The Netherlands

Tom Gunning (Northwestern University)
Evanston, United States

Daan Hertogs (Nederlands Filmmuseum)
Amsterdam, The Netherlands

Nicholas Hiley (British Universities Film & Video Council)
London, England

Frank Kessler (Katholieke Universiteit Nijmegen)
Nijmegen, The Netherlands

Nico de Klerk (Nederlands Filmmuseum)
Amsterdam, The Netherlands

Paul Kusters (Nederlands Filmmuseum)
Amsterdam, The Netherlands

Eric de Kuyper (writer, filmmaker)
Nijmegen, The Netherlands

Sabine Lenk (Koninklijk Filmarchief/Cinémathèque Royale)
Brussels, Belgium

Mariann Lewinsky (Universität Zürich)
Zürich, Switzerland

Angelo Libertini (Centro Sperimentale di Cinematografia)
Rome, Italy

Adrienne Mancia (Museum of Modern Art)
New York, United States

Nicola Mazzanti (Cineteca del Comune di Bologna/Il Cinema Ritrovato)
Bologna, Italy

Don McWilliams (filmmaker, National Filmboard of Canada)
Montreal, Canada

Jeroen van der Meij (Nederlands Filmmuseum)
Amsterdam, The Netherlands

Mark-Paul Meyer (Nederlands Filmmuseum)
Amsterdam, The Netherlands

Philippe-Alain Michaud (Musée du Louvre)
Paris, France

Carlo Montanaro (Le Giornate del Cinema Muto)
Pordenone, Italy

Mario Musumeci (Centro Sperimentale di Cinematografia)
Rome, Italy

Enno Patalas (film archivist)
Munich, Germany

Jennifer Peterson (University of Chicago)
Chicago, United States

Johan Prijs (Haghe Film)
Amsterdam, The Netherlands

Paul Read (Read Associates)
Norfolk, England

Jürgen Reble (filmmaker)
Bonn, Germany

Nicole Renaise (Musée du Louvre)
Paris, France

Thierry Rolland (Pathé)
Paris, France

Heide Schlüpmann (J.W. Goethe Universität)
Frankfurt, Germany

John Sears (Soho Images)
London, England

Carinda Strangio (Stichting Audio-Visuele Antropologie Nederland)
Leiden, The Netherlands

Walter Swagemakers (Nederlands Filmmuseum)
Amsterdam, The Netherlands

Judith Thissen (Rijksuniversiteit Utrecht)
Utrecht, The Netherlands

William Uricchio (Rijksuniversiteit Utrecht)
Utrecht, The Netherlands

Nanna Verhoeff (Rijksuniversiteit Utrecht)
Utrecht, The Netherlands

Ruud Visschedijk (Nederlands Filmmuseum)
Amsterdam, The Netherlands

Herman de Wit (Nederlands Filmfestival)
Utrecht, The Netherlands

Albert Wulffers (filmmaker)
The Hague, The Netherlands